BUTTERCUPS AND DAISY

BUTTERCUPS
AND DAISY

~~~~~~~~~~~~~~~~~~~~~~~~~~~~~~~~~~~~

ELIZABETH CRAGOE

ST. MARTIN'S PRESS
NEW YORK

CONTENTS

ONE

HOW AND WHY

The March sun strikes warmly on the black backs of the cattle, crowding impatiently, behind the gate of the covered yard. Desmond, like a general ordering a battle, gathers his troops around him for the final briefing before the action begins.

'Rachel, take this stick and stand *there* to stop them going up the road. Elizabeth, you run down in front of them, and turn them in at the gate. Matthew, stop them going up the lane to Lan, and I'll let them out and then nip round quickly to stop them straggling away across Llyn Cachy.'

Spring has come again, and we are turning the cattle out for their first bite of grass after the long winter. For three months their world has been bounded by the silage clamps and concrete-covered yards of their winter seclusion. But once again the ancient magic of spring has brought grass to the fields, blackthorn and pussy-willow to the hedgerows. The sun shines hot on the cowshed wall where we lean, discussing our action stations, and it is time the cattle were out.

We take up our positions. Birds sing; the March wind nods the daffodils in the hedgebank; an aeroplane passes. Here comes a milk-tanker lorry, labouring up the hill; the cows will be skittish with their new freedom—will it pass before they reach the road, or will it meet them head-on, bringing panic and confusion? It passes, just in time. The seething mob of furry black beasts bursts onto the road, which rings beneath their trotting feet. It is only a few yards to the gate, which stands invitingly open onto a field of the freshest, loveliest, jade-green grass.

The tight mob of beasts plunges through the gate and fans out. Mad with excitement, the tiny calves, born during the winter, who have never seen such wide open spaces, spring into the air. Everybody runs. Even the staidest old matrons cannot decide which is more imperative, to snatch a bite of the lovely grass, or to gallop away downhill with the herd, tails lofted over backs

1

like so many black pennants. The bull nearly stands on his head as he bucks, flinging his hind legs high into the air. But he is only three, a comparative youngster; high jinks come naturally to him.

We lean on the gate for a long time watching them as they suddenly realise what is at their feet. The noise of thundering hooves gives way to the juicy scrunch of grazing, and the scent of the torn-off grass drifts up to us on the breeze.

It is at times like this that I sometimes remember the Chinese proverb. 'Be careful what you set your heart on' it warns you, 'for you will certainly attain it.' And, the sun hot on my back, I realise with a fresh thump of delight that I have; I have been one of the lucky ones; I am doing what I want to do. I am a farmer.

What was it that led Desmond and me, no longer young, to exchange our safe and seemingly pre-ordained suburban life for the uncertainty, dirt, and hard work of farming? People are always asking me this question, and it is one I find hard to answer. What amazes me is that the world is so full of people who apparently don't want to be farmers. To me it seems a way of life so blessed with advantages that things like hard work, dirt, and uncertain income are factors of no weight in the assessment. I have always felt drawn to farming, and even as a child, could never pass a farmyard without a quickening of the spirit towards it. So when the opportunity came, I felt no hesitation. Refrain from becoming a farmer when the door of opportunity stood open? I could as easily pass a stream without wanting to dabble in its cressy shallows, or a cat without offering it a hand to rub against.

'But,' people persist, when asking about this period of our lives, 'how is it you weren't afraid to risk it?' What they really mean, of course, though delicacy forbids their phrasing it so bluntly, is how did we have the gall to think that we could get away with it? Farming, after all (they rightly imply) is a skilled job. What made you two almost middle-aged people, urban too, imagine that you could do it just like that? Why, after all (they wonder) do people spend years going to agricultural colleges learning the job? In short, who in the hell did you think you were?

Looking back, I must acknowledge that these interlocutors have a point.

Who, then, were we, when we shook the suburban dust from

our feet and headed west twelve years ago with two children, a mini van, a Basenji dog and a Siamese cat?

Desmond was thirty-eight, and had worked for the past ten years or so for the British side of an American pharmaceutical company. His previous experience had ranged from an early foray into banking, through the army during the war, science at London University, selling, market research, and finally his true *métier*, marketing. Several training trips to the American parent company had added an understanding of business principles to a mind that was already both creative and strikingly objective. Desmond is less obfuscated by inessentials than anybody else I know. He is not deceived by glamour, wishful thinking, or show condition. If you are trying on a dress in a shop for his approval, it's no use pulling it flatteringly over to one side and saying 'Perhaps, if I lost half a stone or so, and just took it in here and here. . .?' If he is buying a horse, he is able to ignore the fact that it has a perfectly symmetrical star on its brow, and a flaxen mane and tail. His eye lights rather on its faulty hocks—a useful attribute for a farmer.

Of Cornish descent, he was brought up in London with a sister and two brothers. Luckily for all of us, they are an intensely practical family, and Desmond seems to know by instinct how to do jobs as diverse as mending a water pump and making a bookcase for the bedroom.

My own breeding, I often think, would have made me a capital hunter if I had happened to be born a horse. My Yorkshire father and Irish mother are both doctors (now retired) and we lived half-way between Leeds and Bradford. Every summer, we decamped for a month, three children, nurse, dog and all, to a farm in the Gower, and it was there that my wish to be a farmer first crystallised.

The war led my parents to send us all to schools in mid-Wales, and I used to go riding at a farm near the school, where my feeling that this was the only way to live was strengthened.

Intending to do a degree in agriculture at Leeds University, I did the required year's practical work on a lovely farm in Shropshire, but before starting the academic part of the course, I changed direction, and ended up reading English at Oxford. A three-month secretarial course, several years on the enquiry bureau of an encyclopedia (during which I got married) and a brief and mutually disadvantageous brush with teaching completed my post-graduate experience up to the time I retired from work to have children.

'Of course, you were lucky,' people often say to us, 'having the money to buy a farm.' A remark which always irritates me a little, because we did not find the money hanging on a bush, or buried in a crock at the foot of a rainbow. We purposely delayed our contribution to the perpetuation of the ·human species so that we could both work and save enough for the deposit on a house. Then, when Desmond's firm moved to a new factory in a new town, we bought one. We bought it in the most conventional way, a new house on a new estate; but ordinary as it was, it was the foundation of our modest fortunes. It was quite a pleasant house, with four bedrooms and about a third of an acre of garden, and it cost what seemed then the dauntingly enormous sum of £4,250. We put down £1,000 and left the rest on mortgage. It seemed at the time fantastically ambitious, but somebody up there was undoubtedly looking after our interests.

See us, then, in our new house, setting fruit-trees in the gravelly soil, and acquiring in due course cat, dog, carpets, car, son and daughter in approximately that order. It all seemed very normal and in many ways adequate, but it left us with a fundamental feeling of uneasiness. It felt hollow, somehow; was this all there was to life? The village used to get up a little fund-raising do every year which was widely advertised as offering 'All the Fun of a Country Fair'. It always grated on me. This wasn't the country. Even though cows grazed up to our back garden fence, this place took its ideas, its standards, from the town. Instead of the old saying much quoted by farmers 'Where there's muck there's money', this place would have said, 'Where there is animal excrement, there will have to be the Public Health Authority.'

Other people's conventionality impinged irksomely too. I was sitting on the lawn one day, playing with the current baby, when a neighbour from two or three doors up the road sidled self-consciously through the gate.

'I hope you don't mind,' she said, when we had exchanged meteorological banalities, 'but I've got a complaint to make.'

Flashing a retrospective glance over my recent behaviour, I couldn't pinpoint anything too anti-social, so with an only mildly accelerated heartbeat, I told her to shoot.

'Well, it's like this,' she said. 'When your hubby goes to work in the morning, he always leaves the garridge door open, and *you* don't shut it, and sometimes it stays open all day. Now reelly, you know, that sort of thing does lower the *tone* of the estate!'

In the cause of peace and good neighbourly relations, I humbly promised to toe a smarter line in future, but my spirit revolted within me, and I thought to myself 'Stupid cow.'

When Desmond came home that eveninig I retailed the incident, and fulminated at length on the empty restrictiveness of suburban life.

'It isn't like that in the *real* country,' I said. 'You're down to basics there. What you have on your mind is whether you can get your hay in before it rains, or which bull to use on your cows. *Real* things that *matter*, not fatuous inanities about "lowering the tone of the estate".'

Desmond pondered for a while. 'Have you ever thought,' he said eventually, 'that if we sold this house, we might have enough money to buy a small farm?'

And that is where it all started. Next day I went to the newsagents, and ordered regular deliveries of the two big farming papers, the *Farmer's Weekly* and the *Farmer and Stockbreeder*. The house had increased substantially in value; properties on the western side of the island had not risen to match. We began to do sums on the backs of envelopes, and discuss possible ways of making a living on the sort of properties we could afford.

At first, we intended to buy a really small place, perhaps five to ten acres, and rely entirely on some intensive enterprise like pig fattening or egg production. Laboriously we worked out costings for various systems of farming, approaching everything the hard way from ignorance, and often falling into the most ludicrous errors. Knowing what we do now, we could easily get hold of up-to-date costings on anything from mink farming to keeping summer visitors; we know who to go to. But then, starting from scratch, we found our way up various ridiculous blind alleys before coming up with figures that made any sense at all.

I produced one red herring from a favourite book in which an agricultural sort of character, who ought to know better, says:

'It takes seven pounds of feed ter make one pound of meat— hog's meat, er chicken's meat, er anybody's.'

Working on this basis and calculating the cost of feed from the grain prices given in the farming press, we produced a budget that showed a loss of about £17 for every pig fattened. In real life, many pig farmers get conversion rates of under 2:1—in other words, the pig put on 1 lb in weight for every 2 lbs of food that it eats. But these false starts were self-eliminating, and as we read more, we gradually got a better idea of what was what.

We had not decided at that stage between pigs and poultry as our intensive enterprise, so Desmond filled the unforgiving minute by writing to various manufacturers of equipment asking them to have their representative call on us. I had to laugh at many a salesman's puzzled look as he got out of his car in our irreproachable suburban cul-de-sac; who in the world could there possibly be round here that wanted to discuss the erection of a 4,000-bird battery unit, or the latest thing in farrowing crates? But we fetched them in, gave them tea and picked their brains. They sent us literature; we read it and compared what it said with what we read in books that we got out of the library. We talked to anybody who seemed to have any information to impart, and read all the farming magazines we could lay our hands on. Gradually, our figures became more realistic, and by the time Desmond felt ready to approach the Bank Manager, he had a five-year plan, complete with budgets, to show him, that would have done credit to the Minister of Agriculture himself.

Luckily for us, the Bank Manager had a brother who was a farmer, and was inclined to lend a sympathetic ear to our request. He loved the budgets; he must have liked Desmond too—and his eye was kindly as he gave his final decision.

'You think you'll have about £5,000 when you've sold your house and paid off your mortgage?' he said. 'Well, I'll tell you what I'll do for you. I'll lend you £6,000, and you can pay it back, so much a month to cover capital and interest, over the next ten years.'

But though this was the green light, we still hesitated a little, and it was perhaps the doctor who gave the final push that sent us spinning into agriculture. Desmond's family has something of a history of rheumatoid arthritis, and before entirely committing himself to so physical a way of life as farming, Desmond thought it prudent to have tests done to make sure it wasn't creeping up on him. These entailed two or three visits to the doctor, a choleric character, and a fairly full unfolding to him of all our problems. Then the results came through.

'Absolutely nothing wrong with you,' affirmed the doctor heartily. 'You can go right ahead.'

6

'I'm glad my joints are O.K.' said Desmond. 'But I wonder if I ought to have some tests done on my heart? I have had a desk job for the last few years, and I do sometimes seem to get pains in my chest.'

'Oh, God our help in ages past!' cried the doctor, bouncing irritably out of his chair. 'There's nothing the matter with your heart, man. The trouble with you is that you can't make up your mind. You keep on talking about being a farmer—why don't you damned well go and *be* one, and get on with it?'

Desmond was outraged. He leapt to his feet, red with wrath. 'All right then!' he shouted angrily. 'I damned well will!'

With which he stormed out of the surgery and put the house in the agents' hands.

I will not dwell on the months we spent looking for a farm and trying to sell our own house. It is a stressful situation to be looking for a place where you hope to spend the rest of your life. Your antennae are always on the stretch. 'Will this be it?' you keep asking yourself, as the car turns into each dilapidated farm entrance. 'Will this be the road home? This oak, this churn-stand, in years to come, the milestones that tell us we are nearly there?' But again and again, you are disappointed. Crumbling houses, poor water supplies, steep land, long farm-roads—we saw them all, and more besides. We made two trips to Wales together, and one to the West Country, and Desmond made one or two solitary forays as well.

Friendly or inquisitive people on farms we walked over were always asking us where we were farming now, and to admit that we were novices was to invite a certain lecture. It was so predictable that it became quite tedious—the expected points ticked off one by one, as if we had never thought of them.

'Farming is very hard work, you know!'

'You'll lose all your money!'

'The country is quite different in winter, you know!'

'You have to be out in all weathers!' And so on, ad such nauseam that we eventually became disingenuous, and invented ourselves a protective past. This saved us a certain amount of trouble, but led Desmond, on one of his lone trips round Devon and Cornwall, into a somewhat equivocal situation.

He had stopped to ask the way to a farm he was going to view, and the farmer in friendly fashion asked him what kind of farming he went in for. 'Pigs mostly,' said Desmond unwisely.

'What breed?' asked the farmer, his face lighting up.

'I like the Landrace myself,' said Desmond, and scarcely were the words out of his mouth when the farmer rushed away, shouting 'Father! Father! Come and meet Mr. Cragoe from Hertfordshire! He's thinking of buying next door, and he's an expert on Landrace pigs!'

Then turning back to Desmond, he said to him:

'I'd like your opinion on a boar I've just bought. I paid quite a price for it, I'd like to know how it compares with the pigs on your side of the country.'

'They took me into the shed with this great creature,' said Desmond, telling me afterwards about this ridiculous experience, 'and I didn't know at all what I was supposed to do—I mean, whether to feel its fat or what. I mean, as you know, I've never been that close to a pig in my life. So I asked the father to make it move over to the other side of the box so that I could get a proper look at it. And then I tried to remember all the things I'd read about pigs in the *Farmer's Weekly*, and I said, "I think he's got the most beautiful hams, but I'd like to see him a shade lighter in the shoulder", and that was a lucky shot, because the man turned to his father, and said, "There! That's what I've been saying all along!" But when I left them, I just drove away, and didn't go to look at the other place at all. I couldn't imagine explaining everything to them, somehow.'

Somewhere along the line, we found that we were beginning to look at bigger places, and in one of our discussions, the Bank Manager said he thought it would be a good idea if we did a little dairying for a few years, to spread the risk, and give us (and him!) something to fall back on if the intensive enterprise didn't work out according to plan. So we upped our sights and began to plod round farms of fifty to sixty acres, and sometimes more.

One of the largest farms we walked was also one of the most grotesque. A handsome but dilapidated house faced south over flat fields, bounded by a stream, while the remaining land rose steeply behind it. A dog barked fiercely when we knocked, but the big unshaven German farmer who opened the door stopped it from rushing out by kicking it back so hard that it thudded against the back wall of the kitchen. Unmoved, he ushered us in, and introduced us to his wife, who spoke no English. 'Is seek,' he explained, and gestured at another man who sat crouched on a broken chair by the dirty table. 'Is neighbour. Is come play cards,'

8

he said. The dark, bare kitchen was heated by a paraffin stove, on which queeked and bubbled a big galvanised bucket of curds. 'For cheese,' our brutish-looking host informed us as he prepared to show us the house.

I have never been in a more desolate place in my life. Only the kitchen, of the downstairs rooms, had any furniture in it at all; upstairs, in each bedroom a black iron bedstead stood on bare boards, with a ticking mattress, no sheets or pillows, and one or two dirty army blankets slung over it. One room had a small frayed strip of linoleum. There was no water laid on to the house, and the lavatory, a primitive sentry-box-type earth closet, was across the yard, which was eighteen inches deep in muck. In the bedrooms, some wallpaper had been hung, but for some reason it was attached to the walls horizontally, and hung in dolorous swags round the corners, spotted with mildew. And yet downstairs in the dairy, the stone table stood covered with a baking to make the mouth water—cakes, buns, shiny continental bread plaits sprinkled with poppy seeds—the work presumably of the sick woman who was still morosely playing cards with the neighbour, and did not look up when we came back into the kitchen.

Our German farmer clearly felt that he had done all that could be expected of him in showing us the house, for he pushed a map into our hands and bundled us out of the door to look at the land for ourselves, unaccompanied. And the land gave you just the same feeling of dereliction and despair as the house. It was littered with dead animals. Sheep lay everywhere, in all stages of decay from the fresh corpse with the crows still busy at its eyes to the scattered bones and wide circle of wool in the grass. In the stream lay a fine cross-Hereford calf, dumped there out of the way, staring up at the overhanging hazels with sightless eyes. We couldn't get away fast enough.

We were staying in a caravan belonging to one of my aunts, which she keeps in the Gower, when we first saw the farm we eventually bought. We found the name daunting at first, and referred to it as 'That Pen . . . place'. We also made mock of the agent's jargon which offered in addition to many other amenities a 'roomy concrete dungstead', a phrase that struck strangely on our urban ears. But when we did finally get round to walking the place, we felt at once that it was more of our mark than any of the others we had seen. Not only was it compact and neat, with dry land in good heart, and reasonably close to the village,

9

but even more important, it was free of that horrible air of dereliction. Harry and Mary Jones who owned it kept everything in apple-pie order. Doors were on their hinges, gates had catches, and a fine crop of potatoes had already been planted in the neatly-tilled garden.

True, it was unromantic. The house and buildings are of red brick, unusual in this area, and I always feel that the yard has something of the prim air of a small Midlands railway station. It would not look inappropriate to see little enamel labels saying 'Waiting Room', or 'Porters Only', on the stable and cowshed doors. The buildings date only from the 1930s; there is nothing pretty about them, and they are totally devoid of charm. But we felt that in its smallness, neatness, and relative modernity, the farm offered us our best chance of overcoming our ignorance, and after a further look round and an exploration of the house, we decided to bid for it.

I didn't go with Desmond to the auction, because of the awkwardness and expense, with the two small children; but from my experience in other, less important sales, I can imagine how his heart banged in his chest until it nearly choked him, and how the sweat sprang out in his brow as the bidding rose.

'Five thousand! Five five! Six! Six five! Any advance on six thousand five hundred? It's against you sir—you're in at the back—come along, gentlemen! Seven thousand! Seven I've got! Right, sir, I'll take two fifty! Seven thousand two hundred and fifty pounds! Any advance on seven thousand two hundred and fifty pounds?' . . . Pause, pause, while your heart tries to jump out of your mouth and your whole past life flashes in front of your eyes . . . and then CRASH! The hammer falls, and you are a farmer.

The auctioneer swept Desmond and Harry Jones off to the pub to have a celebratory drink. Harry solemnly raised his glass to Desmond and wished him luck, but he couldn't keep his little dry smile hidden as he said 'It's not often a man buys a dairy farm to make his living on when he's never touched a cow in his life before!'

When Desmond stepped out into the street, the cheque signed and the die cast, there on the windscreen of his car was a parking ticket. We felt at least it should have been inscribed 'Welcome to Carmarthen'.

Our new farm, a quarter of a mile from the village of Meidrim, and eight from the county town of Carmarthen, covered 58.9 acres of deep, loamy land. The general slope of the land is towards the north-west, and a third of the acreage is too steep for a wheeled tractor to go on it safely. The remainder is sweet, kindly land, the fields divided by tall earth banks with hedges on top of them. There are not many big trees, but a few fine old oaks and ashes overhang the little stream that springs from the bottom of the big slope, or 'Llethr Mawr', as the field is called. Most of the field names refer to matters of contour, with which the original owners of the farm seem to have been much preoccupied. We have Parc y Mynydd, mountain field (quite a flat one, actually), Llethr Mawr, the big slope already referred to, Llethr Ganol (middle slope), Cae Uchaf (upper meadow) and Cae Isaf (lower meadow). Then more prosaically, we have Cae Gwair (hay field), and Parc y Stabl, which I will leave the intelligent reader to puzzle out for himself.

Penllwynplan is a fairly typical holding for this area, with its cowshed for twenty, stable for three, and proportionate accommodation for things like hay and young stock. A newly-built silo-barn was a welcome addition. Water was gravity-fed from two wells, the new well and the old well, with whose whimsical personalities we were soon to become all too painfully acquainted.

On the very day of the sale Desmond met our nearest neighbours, and as we owe them a lot, I will introduce them straight away.

Down the hill towards Meidrim lived Howell Harries and his wife Kate. Howell is a whipcord man, subtle of mind, and boundless in energy, farming traditionally, and keeping his place like a new pin. I often wonder if his heart sank when he realised what total novices had come to live next door to him on the uphill side. If it did, he never showed it, and his and Kate's help was invaluable to us.

Up the hill, on a large farm of 150 acres, lived Elwyn and Norah Davies of Lan. I only hope that some turn of fate will one day give us the opportunity of paying back the endless generosity of these kind neighbours. Any time we have called for help, literally at any time of the day or night (as for a difficult calving) it has been forthcoming; we try to live up to their standard of neighbourliness.

Cousins of Elwyn's, Jameses and Davieses, abound in Meidrim, and its environs, and next but one up the road on Sarnau Farm, is Glyn James, married to Sally, Norah's sister. He too was one of our teachers in more ways than one, for he is an inveterate practical joker, and one of the things we learned from him was to look out!

The other farm with which we have a boundary, Penrheol, was occupied by John and Velda Phillips, but their wet-nursing period to us was limited by the fact that they sold up and moved a few months after our arrival. John and Nancy James live there now, with whom we have always been on friendly and neighbourly terms.

Finally there were Harry and Mary Jones from whom we bought the farm. Luckily for us, they did not move far away, but bought a petrol filling station on the Carmarthen road, from whence they patiently answered the thousands of questions with which we bombarded them for the first few months.

Harry arranged for the dispersal sale of his stock and implements to be held in early May, but we could not move up until the 25th because of some problems in the selling of our house. This was a pity, because in the event, much the best thing would have been for us to have bought his cows, his milking machines, his tractor, his implements, and carried on where he left off. Knowing what we do now, we realise that any one of half a dozen farmers would have been happy to come up and milk the cows for us in the three-week interval before we moved, for the value of the milk alone, without any further payment, but at the time it seemed altogether too much of a favour to ask, and we couldn't see how to arrange it. So Harry's cows found other homes, his little Ferguson tractor chugged its way out of the yard for the last time, and the initials 'I.T.' (for 'Incoming Tenant') were not found in the auctioneers' list of buyers at the end of the day.

Harry and Mary moved out to their filling station, and for three weeks the grass grew, and the wagtails flitted undisturbed across the roomy concrete dungstead. And we in Digswell arranged our removal, exchanged our car for a mini van, scrubbed the house down and finally arranged a jam jar of flowers on the landing window-sill as a welcome to our own Incoming Tenants. Then we piled the cats, dogs and children into the van, and set off in the rain for our new life.

TWO

HAYMAKING

The house was long, low, and echoing, and our meagre furniture looked forlorn on its dusty boards. But outside was lovely. No stock had grazed there since the farm sale, and the place had been heavily mucked. We walked round the wet edges of the fields, heavy and silvery with shooting grasses, red clover, sorrel, butter-cups—all the expected wild flowers—and tried to identify some of the grasses in our crop. Timothy was easy, with its twisted leaves and furry cats' tails, and cocksfoot has an unmistakable flower-head. There was a little rye-grass, but the bulk of the sward was formed of a loose-flowered grass like a miniature oat, which the local people discouragingly called 'empty pockets'. This grows quite well in the early part of the year, and brings a fair bulk to the hay crop, but it is slow to re-grow in the after-math, and shows little response to fertiliser. Nobody could call it a desirable constituent of a sward, but until we could re-seed round the farm, we had to make the best of it.

From the point of view of country delights, we could not have chosen a better time for taking over the farm. The year's cycle of growth was at its peak; bluebells and orchises grew among thick tufts of dog-violets on the banks, orange-tip butterflies fluttered from flower to flower, and in alternate sun and rain, the mowing grass grew while you looked at it.

There were birds everywhere. Swallows' eggshells, crimson freckled on white, littered the clean stone floor of the cowshed. Larks sprang up from underfoot in every field; and in the long wet grass by the stream, we found a damaged young buzzard who could not fly. He was about half-grown, and fully feathered. What was the matter with him we never discovered, because he evaded our efforts to catch him, menacing angrily with a still yellow-cornered beak, and glaring with wild tragic eyes. He finally hid himself in the thick hedge-growth of Howell's field, and Howell, finding him dying later in the day, knocked him on the head and slung his body into a clump of nettles.

Buzzards are common birds round here, breeding on this farm and the next, but they do no harm, and as far as I know, nobody molests them. Their enemies seem to be the carrion crow and the raven, who buzz them like fighters. Many a time I have seen a young buzzard, mewing piteously, being forced to circle higher and higher by a pair of crows, diving at it repeatedly until often they drive it right out of sight. My sympathies are always with the buzzard, unfairly, no doubt. It too is a predator, and probably tries hard enough to steal the crows' nestlings if it sees a chance. The raven is hated by buzzard and crow alike, and a sidelong blow in mid-air from his pickaxe beak may well have been our young buzzard's downfall.

When we came out of the house in the early mornings, we would stand on the step for a minute or two just to listen to the silence. There were sounds: birdsongs, the rustle of the wind in the leaves, a cock crowing three farms away down the valley; but through it and over it all was this deep, cool stillness.

There was a sweetness in the air too that we noticed all the time in those early days. You could identify the scent of bluebells in the lane, and hawthorn in the hedgerows, but there was another more astringent smell. I had come across it before, on mountains and in wild places, and it always seemed the very essence of fresh air. I thought at first that it was a composite scent of earth, sap, and rain, but eventually an advisory officer from the Ministry of Agriculture showed me the source of it; a small, neat-flowered grass with the lovely name of Sweet Vernal. It is not at all rare. Dried, it adds a special bouquet to meadow hay, and its living flower pervades the whole countryside with freshness.

And now the weather improved, and we began to worry about making our hay. We had both read a lot about haymaking. We would have been quite well able to keep our end up in a discussion on the relative advantages of square and round bales, or of barn drying as opposed to tripoding; but the decision before us was much simpler: when to cut? We knew that grass cut in the flowering stage, before the seed is really set, makes hay of much higher protein value than older material, but the pollen was shaking in clouds over all the fields of Meidrim, and everybody's mowers were still firmly in the barns. Surely it was not for us, the totally inexperienced, to lead the way? The last days of May passed in brilliant sunshine, and we fretted with indecision. The climate of West Wales is a rainy one; were we perhaps squandering the only fine spell of a patchy summer? We did not cut in May; the decisive factor in the end was that we had as yet no tackle.

Buying a tractor and a complete set of haymaking implements takes a lot of thinking about, and luckily for our peace of mind, June set in with rain, sheets of rain, curtaining incontinently from the south-west, drenching, flattening, bowing down the hawthorn blossom on the hedge until the flowers were brimming, and you looked at the tiny pink stamens as if through a magnifying glass.

So we set about equipping ourselves for the approaching haymaking. We got leaflets, we asked questions, we interviewed representatives. Mistrusting our inexperience, we had decided to resist the temptation of saving money by buying second-hand at farm sales. Retrospectively, I think this was not a bad decision. Until you have used a farm implement quite a lot it is difficult to know where the points of wear will come in it; and even experienced farmers think it no shame to ask a friend who is particularly good with machinery to cast an eye over a prospective buy at a farm sale, to see if it is too worn out. New things come with their guarantees, and in the event we found the firms who sold tackle to us were quite kind and helpful.

The one area in which we were not given the right advice was in buying a tractor. Should we go for a large, a medium, or a small? we asked. Nearly everybody wanted to know what acreage we were farming, and then recommended a medium sized tractor, say forty horsepower. If anyone were to ask us the same question now, we should have no hesitation in recommending a large tractor—65 hp or more. The amount of land you are farming is irrelevant, really. The point is that there are things your big tractor can do, situations it can deal with, that your small one can't; it never happens the other way round. A small tractor works well enough in good conditions, but being lighter and smaller-wheeled, it has not the grip of the big one. The Fordson Super Dexter we bought often got stuck in mud that the big Nuffield we have now doesn't even notice. The difference in cost between them eleven years ago was only about £150, but it is worth more than that to have the power there when you want it.

As well as the tractor, we bought a Ransome cutter-bar mower, and a bizarre-looking object called a Vicon-Lely Acrobat, which claimed to be able to do absolutely everything else with hay except eat it. It would ted, spread, siderake, or windrow, according to the way you adjusted it. It worked well, and it looked like something out of *Dr. Who*. I was glad to identify it when it tripped off the lorry, because I had often seen its brothers in people's barns, and had been too proud to admit that I had no idea whether they were used for sheep-dipping or turnip-hoeing. It was mostly made up of wheels—great, spidery wheels four feet in diameter, with the spokes continuing to form long bent fingers which flick the hay about. It is unusually light for an agricultural implement, and trots springily across the fields behind the tractor on its slender fingers, rather like a thoroughbred foal. It was resplendent in scarlet and cream; the tractor and the mower were royal blue. We did not buy a baler; it is cheaper to get someone to bale for you on contract.

During a brief dry spell early in June, one of our neighbours started to cut. He had ten acres lying in the swath when the rain came down again. For ten days it rained, and the grass lay there bleaching on top and blackening underneath, and we often said we felt sorry for him. 'Unless,' said Desmond, 'it's a delicate mark of friendship. You never know, he may have done it on purpose to make sure that we won't be the only ones to make fools of ourselves this hay harvest.' But for political reasons, we kept this theory to ourselves.

At last the rain cleared, the sun shone, and the wise men in the village square said to each other, 'There's weather in it this time, boys.' The subdued chattering of distant mowers filled the air, and on every farm you could see an ant-like figure on a tiny tractor creeping patiently round the dark hayfields, leaving an ever-widening ribbon of the paler, cut crop.

Our tractor had arrived on a lorry and been driven down ramps to the ground with the mower already mounted on the hydraulics. We chose for our first efforts the most concealed of our fields, but the farm is set on a hillside above the village, and nowhere is really private. What we were about to do had to be more or less in the public eye, so we set about it, and hoped for the best.

The offset cutter-bar mower sticks out behind the tractor and to the right, so the obvious direction to cut a field is clockwise. I remembered, though, that Gwill, my hero when I was thirteen, used to 'open' a field by doing a couple of circuits anti-clockwise, with the mower sticking out towards the hedge. Otherwise there would always be one tractor breadth round the outside that did not get cut. So, acting on this principle, we removed the blade cover, let down the cutter bar, and started.

To begin with, Desmond clattered away in fine style. The chattering knife sheared sweetly through the toppling wave of grass and the swath board laid it over on its side; but before even one circuit of the field was completed, it became apparent that something was wrong. Instead of keeling over behind the mower, the swath began to bundle up on the knife, falling off unwillingly in tangled lumps instead of a neat ribbon. Desmond got down again and again and cleared it, but always after five or six yards, the knife clogged again. For about two acres we struggled on, assuming that it was our fault, but when we were finally driven to send for a mechanic from the mowing machine people, he found that there was a fault in the equipment. When he had put that right and made a few adjustments, it worked quite well.

There were hazards, of course, Parc y Stabl, the first field we mowed, had been the site of the farm sale, where the implements had been laid out, and various unsaleable oddments had been left behind. The grass had grown up over and through them before we arrived, and all sorts of things were effectively hidden. A chain harrow in one corner was firmly anchored by the growth of grass and clover through it, but luckily the purchaser came to collect it before we started mowing, and even more luckily, he had some idea of whereabouts to look for it. Dragging it out made a terrible mess of the mowing grass, and we were not too pleased at the time, but the sward soon recovered. The nearest brush with disaster came when Desmond just skimmed the end of four great baulks of timber lurking on the outermost edge of the swath. Had he mowed into them, nothing could have saved the mower from destruction.

A different kind of hazard, impossible to avoid, was harming the wild animals in the field. I was busy with the brand-new pitchfork, trying to spread a tangled lump of grass into some semblance of a swath, when Desmond stopped the tractor and called me over. He sounded full of distress. 'Look at that mouse,' he said. 'I'm afraid I've damaged it.' The mouse certainly looked damaged. It lay on its side, panting, and staring with round black

17

eyes. 'Could you kill it?' he asked, so summoning up all my reserves of objectivity, I did. At first I felt bad about this, but when you come to examine the options of death for a field mouse, perhaps euthanasia doesn't rate too badly. How do they die? Cat, weasel, owl, buzzard, kestrel; for the lucky ones who survive the attentions of the predators, presumably only senility and starvation. We may have killed several mice in our haymaking, because later when we were baling, we found a number of empty mouse nests, but perhaps luckily that was the only one we actually saw.

Of course, our first mowing did not escape comment, which drifted back to us gradually. 'Have you seen him at Pen'nplan mowing? Started the field wrong way round, and now he's going at fifty miles an hour! Give him six months!' (They were always giving us six months.)

Mowing is a job that every farmer does for himself in this area, as is the subsequent tedding and conditioning of the crop. But baling and carrying the hay are communal efforts. It is vital in this wet and changeable climate to get hay under cover as soon as it is baled, and certain farms, by traditional arrangement, work together on this, bringing together all the tractors, trailers, and labour, and going round from one farm to another as each field comes ready.

We found that we had inherited a place in the team that comprised us and our two main-road neighbours, Pen-y-Bont and Penrheol. John Penrheol had a baler, and did the baling for all three farms at five pence a bale, a price which paid for the twine and showed him a modest profit; and as well as the three farmers and their employees, if any, there were always a few men from the village glad of the chance of a couple of pounds and a free supper. Most farmers were liberal with bottled beer in field and barn when carrying hay, and that too helped to attract casual labour. Hay was usually baled in the late afternoon and evening, when it came fit after its last day's drying, so men with non-farming jobs would join in at the carrying. In a district like this, every male seems to be born knowing how to drive a tractor and pitch bales.

As the junior partner in this scheme, Desmond tended to come last, and he had helped in several fields on the other farms before they arrived in force to carry Parc y Stabl. For a man new to farming the hardness of the work involved in carting bales was a revelation. Freshly baled hay weighs about fifty pounds a bale,

18

and comes off the field at least a hundred bales to the acre. Carrying ten acres meant handling a thousand bales several times, putting them onto the trailer, throwing them off at the stack, loading them onto the elevator, and finally building them neatly inside the barn. Small wonder his hands were often actually bleeding in those early days as he dragged himself up the stairs to bed at half past eleven. Work would often go on, to finish a field from say 6.30 in the evening until half-past ten. It was standard practice to bring in the last few loads by tractor headlights, and many of the bales had to be lifted head high in the course of loading. Three weeks of this, coupled with early rising for milking, took its toll of the strongest, and most of the men were red-eyed and touchy by the time the winter's feed was in the barn.

Sometimes quite young boys would come to help and I remember one child of thirteen sitting at the supper table at 11 p.m. so green with fatigue that I really thought it was a toss-up whether he would be sick or faint. He did neither, however; the next evening he was at it again on another farm, labouring away with the best of them. There are great reserves of resilience in the human frame.

This late-night supper after carrying hay is always provided by 'the Missis' of the farm concerned, and we found that it was an absolutely standardised meal. Cold ham, salad and tomatoes, with lots of ready-cut bread and butter and cake is accompanied by vast quantities of sweet tea. The only other acceptable meat seems to be beef, cooked until it is brown all through. I once made the mistake of serving the cold beef pink—perfect, as I thought—but it was regarded with horror by the helpers, who pushed it with one accord to the sides of their plates.

Parc y Stabl was safely in the barn, and with the weather still holding good, we addressed ourselves to the second of our four hayfields. We had, of course, taken the mower off the tractor to use the acrobat, and now we found to our chagrin that we had the utmost difficulty in re-attaching it. The mower was a solid affair, weighing perhaps three or four hundredweight, of an uncompromising shape, and hopelessly bloody-minded. It was supposed to be attached to the three-point hydraulic linkage at the back of the tractor, but although you could identify the three points on one that were supposed to marry with the three points of the other, no power on God's earth seemed to be capable of bringing them close together. We backed the tractor up from various angles, but still the various pins and holes seemed to bear no apparent relationship to one another. Brochure in hand, Desmond twiddled little handles and let out little screws, but the net result was like the old song: 'We pushed the damper in and we pulled the damper out, but the smoke went up the chimney just the same.' We eventually got one pin in, and I said, 'Why not try raising the hydraulics—perhaps it will drop into place, and we can slip the other pins in.' But as at the touch of a lever the tractor exerted its powerful lift, the mower rose sickeningly from the ground and dangled impossibly askew from its one support, threatening to crash to the ground any second. It took us two shameful hours of a bright June morning to attach that mower in the end, and our efforts might best have been described in terms of the definition of surgery—a combination of brute force and bloody ignorance.

As we got more used to farm machinery, we came to realise that you just don't handle a four hundredweight implement like a lawn mower, and you aren't even meant to. Kicking obdurate hitch pins, or hitting them in with a hammer is everyday stuff; you don't expect these hefty lumps of steel to fit together clunk click every trip. Also, you get the arms of your three-point linkage adjusted to the right length for your particular implements, and the final beam of light dawns when you realise that it is much easier to take the brake off the tractor and roll it the last inch or two up to the mower than to try and push the mower along the concrete to the tractor.

I have never gone beyond the beginner class in handling the tractor, but after a brief experimental period, Desmond, who had driven lorries with gun-trails and so on during the war, became a good tractor driver. He came in for a bit of mockery for a year or two, though, and I remember Dai coming home in a fine state of indignation one evening. 'You know that old Dennis?' he said, naming a man from the village, not a farmer. 'He is saying that you are driving the tractor like an old hen! Cheeky bugger!'

Haymaking in fine weather is hard work, but at least it is full of satisfaction. The slowly filling barn, the ever-steepening angle of the elevator, the smell of the fresh hay sweating, gradually maturing into the poignant sweetness of the cured crop, bespeak a hard job done well, an achievement. But there are years when you judge the weather wrong, and get all the hard work with none of the satisfaction. Hundreds of acres may be mowed in the county, some still in the swath, some almost ready for baling, when the rain starts. The normal procedure round here is to mow, and leave the grass in the swath as it falls for twenty-four hours, to dry the top. Then it is turned, and aerated with several subsequent teddings until it is considered safely dry, which usually takes about three days of fine weather. Finally it is windrowed, or put into fairly substantial stripes ready for the baler, and as soon as it is baled, it is carried to the barn. But if the weather turns against you, you can break your heart trying to dry your crop while a string of depressions play catch-as-catch can with your efforts. Time and again you hitch up the tedder and turn the hay in a bright spell, only to have it snatched back to square nought by a heavy shower. Day by day the quality of the stuff deteriorates, moulds grow, and clouds of dust follow the tedder. What you finally bale and carry is dark, brittle and savourless, full of the dust that gives men farmer's lung; hardly worth sweating for. But as Glyn says, 'If we see a bit of hard weather this winter, you'll find it's better than snowballs.'

There are various ways of speeding up haymaking, and some are used on a few farms, but most have disadvantages of one sort or another. Tripoding, where the hay is built into large cocks or pikes on frames, is one of the most foolproof methods, but it is too demanding of labour for today's economic climate. Barn drying where hot or cold air is blown through the half-dried crop in the barns is favoured by some farmers, but the capital outlay is not trifling, and the hay has to be rather loosely baled to let the air get through it, which makes it awkward to handle later.

Sometimes the weather never lets up at all, and some hay is not baled. There it lies in the field until either the farmer drags it into a heap to rot, or the aftermath grows up through it. Such a year was 1974, with corn as well as hay going to rot on fields too sodden to bear the weight of the tackle needed to harvest it. But in the nature of things, you don't cut all your fields at the same time, and it would be an unlucky man indeed who lost his whole crop in any one year.

Deciding when to bale can be as worrying as deciding when to mow. Take it too soon, and the hay will sweat itself mouldy in the barn, or heat up, even to the point of spontaneous combustion. Leave it a little too long, and you may live to regret it. I remember a field of ours that was almost fit to carry, but wanted

21

an hour or two's sun for perfection. Thinking to play safe, I telephoned the weather man at Rhoose airport and asked about the prospects. 'You should be all right for at least twenty-four hours,' he said confidently. 'There isn't a depression in sight.' So we left the hay overnight, and when we awoke next morning to the thick, relentless mizzle known as 'Swansea Bay rain', I was as mad as a wet hen. I telephoned him again, and asked, 'Where was this little lot yesterday when you told me there wasn't a depression in sight?' 'Madam' he replied haughtily, 'we deal in forecasts, not prophecies!'

So really, with forecasting, as with so many other things, you have to take your own responsibilities. 'There's rain in it' farmers will say to one another when the gnats are biting in the morning. With fifty inches a year to anticipate, most of the weather signs here are rain signs. A ring round the moon means rain—the further away from the moon is the ring, the nearer is the rain; crystal clear horizons mean rain, and paradoxically, so does a curious grey smoky look across the valley. A pale delicate air in the landscape, with all the colours faded, means a good spell of dry weather—we call it the 'Water-colour look'. But the best weather prophet in the district for a long time was a peacock who lived at Pant Farm. His raucous voice could be heard, surely a mile away, foretelling bad weather, and he was always right. The Welsh people averred that he was screaming 'Glaw! Glaw!' which is the Welsh for rain, and it did indeed sound like it.

Various individuals have their own weather signs. Elwyn, our next door neighbour up the hill, for instance, will never cut a field of hay unless a certain patch at the bottom of his yard is dry. But the most consistent judge of the weather we have ever known was our other neighbour, Howell Pen-y-Bont, now retired. He lived beside us for eleven years, and made his four fields of hay each year. Out of those forty-four fields of hay, I only saw him spoil two, and they were not very bad. To walk into his stackyard during the winter was to enjoy the whole essence of successful haymaking—the sweet, nutty smell, the closely-packed golden barns, and the corollary of fat, contented cattle in the cowsheds. It would not be fair, though, to attribute this consistent success to luck. He not only judged the weather well, he also worked early and late on his crop, and all his family worked with him. Many and many a time I have heard him mowing grass, singing at the top of his powerful voice, at five o'clock in the morning, and seen the tractor headlights blazing as the last load creeps home at eleven at night.

Some fields are considered locally to have a jinx on them for haymaking. The hilliness of the land means that any flattish field must be used for hay every year—there can be no question of using fields in rotation. So seeing the same fields cut year by year, one can assess their luck with the weather, and decide if there is any foundation in the jinx theory. Two fields in Meidrim have a name for always getting rain on them after they are cut: Parc South, which borders our garden, and Y Groft, down in the village. It is a fact that during the eleven years we have been here they have only been taken in perfect condition once each, but perhaps a possible explanation is that they are rather large fields by our standards round here, and consequently take longer to bring in.

One way and another, we made three of our four hayfields that first year, and embarked on the fourth. The crop by now was really strong, thick and tangled, and in places laid over by the wind. Desmond was struggling to mow it and having a good deal of trouble with the mower blade clogging, when to his amazement another tractor turned into the field and began to mow behind him. A moment later, two more figures appeared— Lyn Thomas, of Pant Farm, and his brother Edward. 'We could see you were having rather a job with this lot,' said he, 'so I just told my son Herbert here to come up and give you a hand. If you get rain in the bottom of a thick crop like this, you'll never get it dry.' Mr. Thomas's experience quickly solved Desmond's difficulty with the clogging mower, too. He explained that very ripe grass is hard enough to take the edge off a mower blade in one circuit of a field; then he produced a spare blade, and he and his brother sat on the bank, sharpening blades with a file, and calling in the two tractors for a blade-change after each trip round the field. This very practical kindness made all the difference to the work, and eventually we were able to carry the field in good condition.

Working on the hay on Sundays is a matter of conscience, and there is a wide diversity of opinion about it in the district. We have always felt that it was tempting fate to leave dry hay out once it was ready, but one farmer who sometimes baled for us had so strict a principle on the matter that if the hay had been touched at all on a Sunday—mowed, turned, anything—he would refuse to do the baling. Luckily, some were less scrupulous. We never noticed the Almighty making any special dispensations for those who risked their crop in His name; but then, He is notorious for raining equally upon the just and the unjust.

By and large, most farmers hate haymaking. The anxiety of the decisions gets greater over the years as the price of hay goes up. Good hay, which could be bought for about £10 a ton when we started farming, was changing hands at £100 last year, so at the standard rate of 100 bales to the acre, you may be throwing away the best part of £1,000 if you thoroughly misjudge a ten-acre field.

I used to fancy myself as a weather prophet, having always been interested in country lore, and being familiar with about a hundred sayings and jingles on that difficult subject. But a few years ago I was punished for my hubris, and cut down to size in no uncertain way. Desmond was very much in two minds about cutting Parc y Mynydd, a heavy-yielding eight-acre field, and asked me what I thought. I looked at the sky—grey and cool, with high, thin cloud; checked the wind—light and steady, due north —and gave it as my opinion that it would simply have to go on being dry for several days at least. The north, generally speaking, is our most reliable quarter for dry weather, and the south-west for rain. So we mowed the field; and it began to rain, still blowing from the north; and it rained torrentially from that quarter for the next nineteen days. I think that was the most disgusting field of hay we ever carried, and as I tottered across the barn with each nasty bale, I felt strongly that the weather gods had cheated. But I don't go round telling people what a successful weather prophet I am any longer.

Everybody can see the hard work of carrying hay, but tedding looks nice and easy, a doddle, in fact. It can be delightful on a bright day, but it is never quite as relaxing as it appears. Modern tedders are driven from the tractor's power-take-off, and you have to keep glancing back all the time to make sure that they are working all right. Any part snapping off as the heavy machine bounds over the dry hard field may fall into the working parts, and be forced through by all the power of the tractor's sixty-five horses in the blink of an eyelid; and there you are, in the middle of the field, with your crop waiting to be turned, and your tedder smashed to bits.

Visitors often wonder why the men round here so rarely work with their shirts off. But there is method in it. 'Sit on a tractor for two days without your shirt in this sun,' they say, 'and then try to carry bales on the third day. There's sore your back will be.' So they leave the visitors to do the sunbathing, and only get tanned themselves on faces, necks and arms.

As wages in other jobs have improved, non-farming men in the village have become less and less keen on labouring in the hay-fields. It is no rare sight these days to see a frantic farmer with hay ready to bale driving round the village, going into the pubs, asking—begging, even—for help, and meeting with nothing but excuses. You can't blame the men. It is hard work in the hay on top of a regular job, and nowadays they don't really need the extra money, but it is hard on the farmers and their families. For if you can't get any help from the village and all your neigh-bours are busy, you simply have to set to and do it all yourself. And making hay without adequate labour is a deadly grind. The tractor parts of the operation are not too laborious, but when it comes to carrying, your hundred-odd bales an acre must be lifted onto a trailer, humped into position on the load, thrown off at the barn, humped onto the elevator, dragged across the stack (the footing all uncertain) and packed tightly into their final positions.

Building a stack, even with baled hay, is a skilled job. There is a certain amount of variation in the size of the bales even from the same baler, and in any case, the size of the bales is not always an exact multiple of the size of the barn. So you have to fadge a bit, leaving a hole, perhaps, which you hope to cover up in the next layer. The edge must be tied in, too, with bales running counter to the others, lest a whole block sag away, and crash down as the hay sweats and settles. I have never been a good stacker, but you do learn a few tricks by watching others, and at least my stacks don't fall down. Desmond is much better, having a straighter eye for a line, as well as more strength and experience.

But when you have to carry and stack the hay without enough helpers, you hurt so much before the end that you wish you could lie down and die. The bale-strings hurt your hands; the cut ends of the hay scratch your arms and legs; and the heaving and lifting of load after remorseless load makes you wonder whether what you've really got is a slipped disc, a hernia, or a heart attack.

Being a woman, I have seldom been required to labour to this extremity, but I am sure the men too find it hard, and are kept going largely by pride. But this is a proper pride, which leads to achievement, and I have often admired the spirit that leads a man to slog on, galvanising his weary helpers to efforts they never thought they could make, and refusing to admit even the possibility of giving up until the last load is safe under the barn roof. Then at last the insistent racket of the elevator is stilled, the chuntering tractors switched off, and the men clatter into the kitchen for supper, blinking at the brightness, and almost too stiff and weary to talk. Supper is eaten quickly, for everyone is longing for bed; then it is 'Nos da, boy'—'Diolch yn fawr— nos da!' and the car headlights scything a path of brightness through the narrow lanes on the last lap home.

A climate as wet as this can make haymaking a traumatic business, and more and more people are turning to silage for the bulk of their conserved feed. A certain amount of hay will always have to be made, for calves and so on; but most of us, asked for our opinion on haymaking, would have no hesitation in saying:

'Hay? Nonny, no!

THREE

COWS FOR BEGINNERS

Of course one of the first things we had to do, even before starting on the hay, was to assure ourselves of an income. And an income on a farm of this size round here means dairy cows.

There are five breeds of pure dairy cow milked in this country —the Ayrshire, the Dairy Shorthorn, the Guernsey, the Jersey, and the British Friesian. Each has its supporters, fanatical in defence of their own breed, but it cannot be an accident that something like 90 per cent of the national herd is composed of Friesians. They are those big black and white ones that you see everywhere. They are the farmer's breed *par excellence*, yielding more milk on average than other breeds, and providing a splendid beef animal to boot. Thus, bull calves, any heifers not wanted for breeding, and superannuated cows (known as 'barreners') can find a profitable end in the roasting tin or pie dish. Quality of the milk is lower than in the Channel Island breeds, but normally good enough to pass the minimum standards imposed by the Milk Marketing Board, which are 3 per cent fat, and 8.5 per cent other solids not fat. When the Friesians were first imported into this country from the Continent in the early 1920s (in large numbers—nobody can exactly pinpoint the very first importations) Shorthorn breeders used to circulate snide jokes about the poor quality of Friesian milk. 'Why buy a water cart when you've got fifty pedigree Friesians?' they would ask one another, falling around with laughter. But careful breeding has eliminated that fault from the modern Friesian, and several pedigree Friesian herds near here actually have a butterfat average of over 4 per cent, which is the legal minimum for Channel Island (gold top) milk.

We should undoubtedly have bought Friesians for our first cows, but here we fell into a failure of communication, and made a mistake as a result of both being so frightfully decent to one

27

another. The farm on which I had long ago been a pupil in Shropshire had had Ayrshires (brown and white cows with big horns, originally from Scotland) and Desmond thought I wanted to have them again. This led him in the goodness of his heart to talk about them so much that I thought *he* wanted them. The result was that we bought Ayrshires instead of Friesians against the better judgement of both of us and one of our favourite hindsight themes begins 'Suppose we'd bought Harry's Friesians at his dispersal sale.'

When you set out to buy a herd of dairy cows, several options are open to you. You can buy at dispersal sales, you can bid at the weekly cattle markets around the country, or you can put yourself in the hands of a dealer. To begin with we chose the latter course, and although our farming acquaintances predicted dire things, we actually acquired some very nice animals at a reasonable price, and with some sort of a guarantee.

Many big cattle dealers offer dairy cows in different categories of yield at different prices. Three to four gallon cows are cheap (and so they should be!); four to five gallon cows are a bit more; and five-gallon-and-over cows will set you back a little above the market average. But the guarantee holds good, and you can at least be sure that the animal you buy is capable of starting with the prospect of a fair yield, though she may not maintain it. If you buy in the open market you have no redress if you find that the animal is only giving a gallon a day when you get her home, provided that her udder is healthy and that veterinary examination proves her to have calved recently. So, guarding against the worst effects of our ignorance, we settled for ten of the best to start with, and never had any cause to regret it.

Large scale dealers, advertising on a national scale, have agents buying for them at all the major cattle markets in the country. Freshly-calved cows are bought when they can be had at a reasonable price, and trucked to the big home farm—at Shrewsbury in the case of our dealer. There they are milked for a few days and put into production categories, and customers can either come and choose among them, or they can be ordered, unseen, by telephone.

Desmond went up to Shrewsbury one day about a week after we arrived at the farm and chose our ten. They were to be delivered the next day, and we spent an exciting afternoon assembling our super brand-new stainless-steel milking machines, so stiff and heavy, and re-scrubbing the already perfectly clean cowshed ready for their arrival.

We had already prepared a list of names to be apportioned among them. I have never much liked animals having people's names, and we finally decided on a botanical theme. Many of the nice old traditional cows' names are flower names—Buttercup, Daisy, and so on. We riffled through our Collins wildflower book and listed our favourites. It seemed a fruitful source—enough names were there, surely, for a lifetime of cowkeeping, and we envisaged ourselves, old and bent, nearing the end of the book:

> Cusha, cusha, cusha calling—
> Come up Whitefoot, come up Lightfoot,
> Come up Tubular Water Dropwort . . .

and then the lorry was turning into the yard, the ramp thumped to the floor, and down they clattered thankfully into the cool of the cowshed. The lorry-driver helped us to fasten them up with their heavy polished neckchains, then away he went, and we were left to face our first milking.

I am ashamed to acknowledge that it took us an hour and a half to milk those ten cows the first time. I had milked for a year in my pupilship, but seventeen years of amnesia lay between me and that, and although Desmond had had a few preparatory lessons on a farm in Hertfordshire, he was hardly an expert. The cows, nervous from the strangeness of it all and aware of our ineptitude, started and sidled. One big roan, christened Heather, kicked a bit, but I remembered the trick for that—a rope, tied tightly round the body, in front of the udder—and we finally succeeded in extracting the milk. Then we had to strain and cool it, and wash the utensils in our brand-new galvanised dairy sink.

How proud we felt of those cows, distinctively brown and white among all the surrounding herds of magpie Friesians. How we admired the sleek sides, the full bags, the swinging silken tails, as we brought them down to the cowshed for morning and evening milking. Some of them were with us for years and left offspring to keep the names alive—Cherry-plum, Holly, Rowan, Heather, Meadowsweet, Mistletoe and Bracken.

Having to have the milk churns on the stand to catch an early lorry we used to get up early in those days. It seemed no hardship to us to step out into the cool morning at 5.30, the sun already

29

beginning to climb up the sky, and to walk up the lane through the ringing birdsong to fetch the cows. The one of us who wasn't fetching the cows would put the milking machines together and put a little ration of cattle cake into each manger so that the cows would go eagerly into their places and be no trouble to tie up. When they were all munching at the same time it sounded like the sea grinding the pebbles together on Dover beach, that 'melancholy long, withdrawing roar' that Matthew Arnold noted.

But we were far from melancholy. The swallows bubbled their chattering song on the rafters, the pulsators on the machines added their rhythmic chunk-chunk! chunk-chunk! and we were happy as we moved from cow to cow, washing the udder with warm water, drawing off the fore-milk into the strip-cup and slipping the teat-cups on, where they stayed by their own suction, as the cow quietly ate her cake. We learned to feel the difference between a full bag, where the outer skin slides over a firm surface, like a taut muscle, and an empty one, which is silky soft, like a suede glove; we weighed each cow's milk night and morning, and adjusted the cake ration accordingly; we turned out quite a creditable amount of milk, and did everything by the book; but we had a lot to learn.

The first lesson came soon enough. I was forestripping Rowan into the strip-cup when I noticed a clot. The strip-cup is a metal mug with a black plastic lid across it, onto which you squirt a little milk from each teat. The milk runs through a little hole down into the mug, but any irregularities show up against the black, and there it was—a small clot of milk, about the size of a lentil. It was our first introduction to the scourge of the dairy industry, mastitis.

Considering that it costs farmers several million pounds a year, mastitis is surprisingly little known outside farming circles. It is a disease of the udder with several causative organisms and is mainly found in machine-milked cows, particularly ones which are heavy yielders. (Perhaps I should add that mastitis in human beings is an entirely different condition.) Highly contagious, it can be spread by flies, by udder cloths, by the hands of milkers, or by the milking machine itself. The first sign is a clotting of the milk, but if this is untreated, inflammation of the udder soon follows which spoils milk production and often permanently impairs the affected quarter of the udder. An acute infection can make the cow quite ill, or even in extreme cases, kill her. So mastitis is not to be trifled with, and recognising this herald of disaster for what it was, we sent for the vet.

I think, looking back, that Mr. Harries, our vet, whose acquaintance we now made for the first time, was rather surprised to be summoned for such an extremely mild and early case of mastitis. Farmers in a dairy district soon learn how to treat these ailments themselves, only calling the vet if the cow seems ill in herself, or does not respond to treatment. But when we explained our ignorance, he was kind and helpful, and showed us what we had to do. Taking a small tube with a long nozzle from a box, he pushed it right up the cow's teat canal and squeezed the contents into the quarter. We were amazed that she allowed him to do this. The nozzle looked so big and the hole in the end of the teat so tiny; but she didn't even break the rhythm of her cudding. Massaging the penicillin briskly around inside the quarter, Mr. Harries explained that we must repeat the treatment night and day for three days, discarding all milk from the affected quarter both during and for forty-eight hours after the treatment. Our hearts were in our mouths that evening when penicillin time came, but imitating Mr. Harries with as casual a boldness as we could muster, we were pleasantly surprised to find how easy it was.

Rowan's mastitis cleared up quickly, but the next dose of trouble was more serious. All the cows were milking quite well, yielding over five gallons each, which was normally given in the proportion of, say, twenty-five pounds at night and thirty-two in the morning. (There are 10.3 lbs of milk to a gallon.) Great was our consternation when little dark Cherry-plum shambled, head down, into her stall one morning, and presented us with a mere four pounds of milk. Shocked, we looked at her with more attention. Her nose was dry, her skin seemed tight over her ribs, her body was hot to the touch, and she hadn't eaten any of her cake. Once again, we rang Mr. Harries.

On his arrival, Mr. Harries gave us a short lecture on the problems of moving cows from one farm to another, particularly one many miles away. Pushing a thermometer with casual aplomb up Cherry-plum's bottom, he told us that different farms can be infected with diseases against which no imported animal necessarily has any resistance. Home-bred stock acquire immunity, literally, with their mothers' milk. Cherry-plum's illness, he told

31

us, was tick-borne fever. 'And I shouldn't be surprised if you find it runs through the lot of them,' he added. It did.

Treatment was a massive injection of an antibiotic and a series of doses to be given by mouth. 'I want her to have one of these in a pint of warm water every evening for the next five days,' he said. 'Ask one of your neighbours to show you how to give her the drench, it's quite easy.'

It looked easy, too, that evening, when we ran out onto the road and stopped John Penrheol who was going home on his tractor, cap pulled right down over his nose against the westering sun. Deftly seizing the cow by her nose, he twisted her head round, and propped her chin up on his knee. Then he guggled the dose, in a squash bottle, into her mouth, pointing out the necessity for making sure that it went over her tongue, not under, and not too fast, lest she choke.

But the following evening when we tried to administer the dose ourselves, we found out exactly why the process of dosing a cow is called drenching. Perhaps it was our lack of skill, or perhaps she was beginning to feel better; anyway, instead of standing there calmly gulping, she stood on her right ear and twisted her head out of reach. When we did manage to insert the bottle into her mouth, she ground her teeth fiercely on its neck and let the liquid run craftily out of the corner of her mouth instead of swallowing it. Then she tried to lie down, rolling protesting eyes at us. In the end, we were all drenched.

The doses worked, and Cherry-plum recovered, but her milk yield never returned to its peak, and as the tick-borne fever ran through cow after cow, the result was a disappointing diminution of our milk income. We decided to buy some more cows.

Curiously enough, none of the second batch of ten cows ever got tick-borne fever, nor has any other cow that we have brought on to the farm. The explanation must be that after the farm's empty weeks the grass was long in the grazing fields. Ticks breed much more readily in rough grass than in short-cropped pastures. By the time the second lot of cows arrived, the aftermaths had grown in the hayfields, short and clean, and the cows were grazing those.

July melted into August. We were now milking twenty cows, and it was time to think about getting the first batch back in calf again. A cow calves, ideally, once a year. Gestation, as for human beings, is nine months. So she should be mated or 'served' three months after calving. After this time, her milk yield will gradually diminish, and most cows are dry for the two months immediately before calving. With the new calf, obviously, comes the new flush of milk, and the whole cycle starts again.

Few farmers keep bulls nowadays to serve their dairy cows; most rely on the Milk Marketing Board's excellent artificial insemination service. A modest charge, painlessly deducted from your milk cheque, buys you a shot of semen from an excellent bull of whatever breed you want, put in the right place by an expert. For a few pounds extra, you can have the semen of any particular bull you care to nominate, and details of the daughters' performance, et cetera, are freely available.

In practice, what happens is that you notice that a particular cow is on heat, or 'bulling'. Cows demonstrate this by indulging in a crude and rather pathetic mating pantomime among themselves; a cow that stands still and lets others 'ride' her is receptive, or 'asking' as one dear old farmer of my acquaintance used to call it. So you ring up your local A.I. centre, whose telephone number is engraved on your heart, before 10 a.m.

'Good morning. Carmarthen Cattle Breeding Centre.'

'Good morning. Mrs. Cragoe, Penllwynplan.'

'What breed, please?'

'Friesian, first time.'

A terse conversation, that should, if all goes well, lead to another calf in nine months' time. 'First time' is important, because if the cow fails to conceive, you get a certain number of free repeat services.

A.I. men, in real life, as in jokes, are always in a hurry, and like you to have everything ready. A bucket of water, warm in winter, a bar of soap, and a towel. The bride is chained up in her stall. The great lover dons a macintosh garment that fastens down the back, and a disposable plastic glove on his right arm. Approaching the cow with the confidence of experience, he shoves his soaped arm right up her bottom, and gropes around, a bemused expression on his face. The cow, who is not infrequently moved to defaecate, arches her back and looks round with a mild air of protest. Suddenly the A.I. man's face beams. He has located the cervix through the bowel wall. Now one quick wipe with a disposable paper towel, and the long narrow syringe is inserted, guided to the right position by the left hand, and the plunger pressed. Then a quick squirt of disinfectant in the bucket

33

of water, a scrub down of arm, boots and apron, and the job is done. All being well, it only takes about two minutes.

Sometimes the cow fails to conceive, and the whole business has to be gone through again. One cow, a super-excellent pedigree cow called Dungleddy Gwen, was inseminated nine times before she finally 'held'. On the last time the A.I. man remarked 'I think we got her this time, there's a drop of milk coming from her.' Dai, who was working with us at this time, was standing up in the stall beside the cow to stop her swinging round her quarters as she was served. 'Where? Where?' he cried, looking up at the ceiling, down at the floor, anywhere but the right place. 'From her tit, you dull bugger' growled the A.I. man, withdrawing soggily. The milk indicated that a spasm of uterus had set off a sympathetic contraction of the mammary system. The heat must have been at a particularly propitious stage, and sure enough, the cow conceived.

The first calf to be born on the farm, though, was not from one of the cows we had inseminated ourselves, but from Clematis, a cow we bought in calf at a sale.

The date was 23 December, and a cold evening, with snarling squalls of rain was succeeding a mild and open day. We felt that the cows were happier out than in, so whenever the weather was clement, we turned them out into the fields for the day. After evening milking, they spent the night in the cowshed.

Anticipating their cake, the cows gathered by the gate as milking time approached. But Clemmie was not there. I rushed to fetch Desmond, and, hearts in mouths, we went to look for her. Ten minutes' search revealed her, looming white through the dusk at the bottom of a little square enclosure where once a cottage stood, still called 'The Garden'. Was she calving? We tiptoed up, straining our eyes in the gloom—and then we both saw it at the same time—a dark, wet wisp of a creature that rose on buckling legs from the ground, and feebly shook its hanging ears. 'It's black!' I exclaimed. 'It's a bull!' cried Desmond. Both were wrong; excitement and the fading light perhaps had something to do with it. It was in fact a little red heifer.

The tiny creature stood, trembling, in the cold, while Clemmie licked it and talked to it in the deep, low voice cows have for their calves. We must get it in, quickly, to warmth and shelter. But how? The place Clemmie had chosen for her accouchement was almost at the foot of the steepest slope on the farm, inacces-

34

sible to any vehicle. The only thing to do was to pick the calf up and carry it to the lane, where we could put it into the mini van. So, taking a deep breath, Desmond seized the little wet thing round the chest and behind the back legs, and heaved. The calf struggled—Clemmie fussed around—and Desmond staggered up the bank with his burden. A new-born calf weighs about eighty pounds, and a slippery, squirming eighty pounds is no light weight up a one in three slope. The blood was roaring in his ears before he reached the lane.

We named the calf Sweet Rocket, and as Desmond bucket-reared her, she grew very attached to him, and remained particularly 'his' cow throughout her life with us. She had one curious characteristic; both ears had an indentation, as if someone had pressed them together like a sandwich, and taken a bite out of them. Having seen her within a very few minutes of her arrival, I can confidently assert that nobody ever did—she was born like it. None of her own calves carried this odd trade mark.

How we fussed over Rocket! Her pen had to be so clean, her milk at so exact a temperature. We bought her a bag of calf coarse mix, a delightful cocktail of flaked maize, crushed oats, bran, and locust beans. The latter were nice to pick out and eat, dry, dark pods, with a sweet, fruity flavour. We had her horn buds removed by the vet when she was about a week old, and he thrilled us by remarking to his assistant: 'I don't know when I saw a nicer heifer calf than this one, George.' We were like new parents, and she was our blue-eyed child.

Perhaps because she was brought up as an 'only', Rocket never acquired a good social manner with other cows. No other calves were born for several months after her, so she was quite big before she had to associate with other animals, and it made her stand-offish. She was not particularly low in the pecking order; if she had to, she could give another beast a pretty telling bunt of the head to establish her precedence; but she liked to keep herself to herself. We kept her long after the other Ayrshires had been replaced by Friesians, and, coming in to milking, she always walked last, a bit apart. We used to say that she was observing a colour bar, and threaten to report her to the Race Relations Board.

Her mother, Clematis, was a wonderful cow, who gave 1,400 gallons of milk in her best lactation, besides presenting us with five heifer calves, including one pair of twins. She calved these late one night, in a loose-box. It was my turn to sit up and oversee the calving, and I was so excited that I woke both Desmond and Dai to tell them the good news. To do them credit, they both had the courtesy to murmur 'Good!' before relapsing into their hoggish slumbers.

It was in keeping cows, more than in anything else, that I found the pleasure I had hoped for in farming. There was satisfaction in the very minutiae of the daily routine, in things like cleaning out the cowshed after each milking. The strong, rhythmic movements of shovelling up muck on concrete pleased me; so did the dexterous flick that scoops up the last spoonful—even the concrete itself, polished by years of brushing, gleamed wet and shining after the daily scrub, like stones in a river bed.

Fetching the cows for milking and taking them back afterwards was a favourite job too. Walking day by day up the same section of deeply-sunken lane, you could watch the changes of the season in the vegetation of the banks. The close tapestry of spring patterned them with leaves—celandine, strawberry, herb Robert and wild violet. Then came 'The year's primal burst of bloom', snowdrops and celandine yielding to bluebells, campion and wood-sorrel. Tall feathery grasses covered the dying bluebell leaves, speared through with towering foxgloves, sorrel, and bracken, which the cows tore off in great mouthfuls as they filed past, releasing spicy gusts of fragrance. Sometimes a goldfinch with a nest in the hedge would flutter from perch to perch in front of us for a hundred yards or more, giving us a rare chance to get a good look at its clown-like red and white face, and the bars of brilliant yellow across its wings. Often when you turned the corner a buzzard would rise from a fence-post, a favourite perch, less than ten yards away, and you could see the barred breast and the pale underwing as it banked round to gain height.

The cows safely through the gate, we would fill their water-trough from a stand-pipe by it, and enjoy the evening light while they all crowded round drinking, until the humblest was satisfied, and the trough full for the night. The cows' personalities were shown in their behaviour at the trough. Big Hawthorn shoved her way to the front, spiking away competition with her horns; Comfrey, at the other end of the scale, scarcely dared to dip her lugubrious face over the rim of the trough, and always sucked the water up with her lips half an inch above the water level, with a lot of noise and effort. Ayrshire cows are renowned for

36

the neatness of their udders, and most of ours were tidily hung, but Comfrey rejoiced in an appendage described by Desmond as a first cross between a shopping basket and a sputnik with hairs on it. Still, handsome is·as handsome does, and a yield of 1,600 gallons in 305 days, her lifetime best, is not to be sneezed at.

It was during the first summer of our farming life that we learned of the curious theory that all cows subscribe to, that where the head goes, the body must necessarily be able to follow. I was calling the cows for milking one afternoon from their pasturage on Cae Uchaf and Llethr Ganol. Having no sheepdog, we relied on calling, and the cows soon realised that the traditional cry of 'Trwy! Trwy! Trwy!' (I still don't know exactly what it means) summoned them to a nice feed of cake in the cowshed, and came willingly enough. Cae Uchaf was inadequately divided from Llethr Ganol by an old and defective fence, part bank and hedge, part rusty barbed wire with several gaps of twenty feet or more along its length. Most of the cows ambled down to the gate sensibly enough, but Clover, finding herself behind one of the barbed wire sections with her herd-mates fifty yards in front of her, panicked, and instead of walking two yards to the left, to the nearest gap, crashed straight through the lethal tangle. Dripping blood, she galloped down to the rest, and shoved her way into her stall where she attacked her cake with relish, oblivious of the ruin at the nether end.

Teat injuries often seem relatively painless when they are fresh, and she stood surprisingly quietly while we sponged away the blood and revealed the extent of the damage. It could have been worse, but to novices like us, it looked bad enough. There were several long scratches on the udder itself and one or two snicks on the front teats. But worst of all, one set of barbs had really caught the back left teat, and a horrid gash shaped like the W.D.'s broad arrow marking sent our hearts into our boots. No milk was dripping out, so we decided not to have the cut stitched. The problem, of course, with a teat injury, is that a dairy cow has to be milked twice a day come hell come high water, and a lot of the body's work in restoring damaged tissues is necessarily disrupted by the pressure and suction of the milking machine. In practice, it means that you have to cause the cow some pain, perhaps considerable, and she endeavours, reasonably enough, to kick you to hell while you are doing it. Leaving milk in the quarter is certain to bring on mastitis of the worst kind, which can lead to a defective quarter the next time the cow calves, or even a completely dry one. Thus, in one stroke, your cow that goes through a fence risks halving her value, for a three-quartered or light-quartered cow is only worth what she will fetch as a barrener, however young and beautiful she may be.

We were lucky with Clover. Although she was really rather a nervous cow, she submitted to having her hind legs tied together for milking, and milked out cleanly enough, though her anguished Charleston showed how uncomfortable it must have been for her. In about a month, the teat healed up, and the dangerous fence was bulldozed out as part of the Great Leap Forward that we now—so erroneously—took.

FOUR

DAI

As we embarked on our second year, we decided that the time was now ripe for us to employ a boy, and began to look around for a suitable candidate. Elwyn, at that time, had as his 'servant-boy' (a local usage that shocked us at first, but which we soon discovered had no connotation of servility) a young cousin of his, Claude. Claude's father had a small farm on the other side of the village—on the opposite lip, so to speak, of the valley to us. Claude's younger brother Dai was working on another farm, but he was looking for a change of job, and it was suggested that we should try to get him.

I well remember the first time he came to see us. Just seventeen years old, and more at home in Welsh than in English, he sat, red and shy, stroking the dog's ears, while Claude conducted the negotiations on his behalf. Dai opened his mouth only to agree to everything that we proposed. He would sleep in? Yes! The work would be mostly with cows, but a certain amount with the hens. Yes! That was all right. Wages, time off, daily hours, were explained. Yes! That was all right too.

So we arranged for him to start the following Monday, a lucky day for us, and I hope not a bad one for him either.

Many of our ways were strange to Dai, but having got over his initial shyness, he breasted them boldly. He disliked our linen sheets, which he referred to as 'those white buggers', so I bought some blue flannelette ones, between which he slept very soundly. Getting him out of them in the morning, indeed, was the one problem. The only reliable method was to drag the bedclothes right off him and physically tumble him out onto the floor. As he slept only in a shirt, I deputed this job to Desmond.

Once awake, he proved a wonderful asset, and our lives became much easier. A farmer's son, he knew things about farming that we had never thought about, and we learned a lot from him. There are simple things like picking up a bale of hay on your shoulder that you do wrong until you see someone else do it right; an ounce of experience is often worth a ton of theory. He loved cows, and showed great skill in handling difficult ones and young heifers. An animal that was 'fidget' through a teat injury, or frightened, could rely on his patience, but he wasn't going to truckle to attacks of temperament. 'You want to shout nasty to them, Missus,' he would tell me when stuggy little Holly kicked the milking machine cluster out of my hand, and sure enough, at his growling 'Gerrup ... you ...' she would stand quiet, looking round at him with mournful, innocent eyes. Not approving of hitting cattle, we kept no sticks in the cowshed, but occasionally Dai would give some recalcitrant matron a great flat-handed clout on the ribs, making her boom like a drum, and producing instant obedience.

Swearing came from him as naturally as breathing, and with as little significance. 'Fuck-aye' was a normal affirmative, and gave his conversation a rather Scottish flavour. People he didn't like fell into two categories, a 'fat bastard' or a 'fucking Jew'. It was of course possible to be both.

He was extremely easy-going about food, accepting as down-right delicacies things that ranked as nursery food with us, like shepherd's pie and bread-and-butter pudding. The food at his previous farm had been one of the chief sources of complaint, as he told us with a good deal of brio. 'There was this pig called Percy. And he was a fat bugger. And he was killed. And after that, every morning, on my plate—fucking Percy! Cold! It was turning on me.' Fat boiled bacon every day for breakfast is not everyone's taste, but the alternative was an even more bizarre amalgam of hard boiled eggs and tinned tomatoes, also cold, straight out of the tin. 'I have been telling her I don't like them, but no good, every morning there is a fucking *bundle* of the buggers on my plate.'

Dai was still somewhat in the hobbledehoy stage when he came to us, and was sometimes clumsy. Desmond used to get particularly annoyed with him if they had to do any work together that involved moving anything heavy—sleepers, say, from a silage clamp. Dai would be sure to drop one of them on Desmond's foot, and then overwhelmed by nervousness, would be unable to restrain his giggles. I got accustomed to rushing out to pour oil on troubled waters when I heard the classic mixture of oaths and laughter. There would be Desmond, hopping round like Rumpelstiltskin on one foot, face as black as thunder, delivering a diatribe against clumsy fools who let things fall on people's feet, while Dai, red with distress, was doubled up in convulsions of helpless mirth.

Dai always enjoyed reading the small-ads column in the local paper, his fancy flitting from prospect to prospect through romantic vistas of ownership. Welsh mountain ponies, spreckle-faced sheep, good working collie bitches, he toyed with the idea of owning them all. Nothing if not generous, he was always encouraging us to share this pleasure. 'Seven peahens, Croes-y-Ceiliog' he would read out. 'You want to get some of those, now, Boss.' or 'Three piece suite and swede drill, as new—that'd be handy for you.' One evening, Desmond happened to have picked up the paper first, and folding it back to 'Miscellaneous' he said 'Here's something for you, Dai—from Ystradgynlais—Twenty-five spreckle-faced servant-boys—you want to get some of those!' 'Where? Where?' cried Dai, peering eagerly in search of this non-existent piece of whimsy. But he enjoyed a joke against himself as much as any other.

It was in the spring of Dai's arrival that we started putting into practice some of our plans for making the farm into a more productive unit. A scheme called the Small Farms Improvement Scheme was in operation then, whereby the state, through the Ministry of Agriculture, subsidised improvements on small farms to the tune of £2,000, a very useful sum in those days. You could take out your money's worth in various ways—in fencing, re-seeding, or draining; you prepared a scheme to suit your own situation, in cahoots with your own advisory officer, and submitted it to the higher powers for approval. Once it was approved, you went ahead and did it, and cheques duly arrived through the post.

We decided to take up all our grant in ploughing and re-seeding all round the farm. The flat fields we could do ourselves, but a contractor with a caterpillar tractor had to be brought in to do the steep slopes.

It does not sound much to plough and re-seed a field, but when we looked into the figures, we were surprised to find how it all mounted up. Preparing the seedbed takes several passes with the tractor—ploughing, rolling, disc-harrowing, chain-harrowing, fertilising, sowing, chain-harrowing again, and finally rolling—in that order—which represents a fair amount of diesel fuel used.

41

The soil is analysed, and recommended dressings of lime, basic slag and fertiliser are applied, all to be bought, while a good seed mixture itself will set you back several pounds an acre.

The technicalities of re-seeding did not cause us any heart-searching, because we did it all under the auspices of our District Adviser, and he worked out the fertiliser requirements and seed mixtures for us. All we had to do was to put his recommendations into practice.

The seed mixtures he designed for us read like some lavish mediaeval recipe:

S. 19 annual ryegrass	4 lbs
Creeping fescue	2 lbs
Wild white clover	1 lb
Timothy	3 lbs
Dutch white clover	1½ lbs
Perennial ryegrass	5 lbs

The idea being to provide a sward of compatible grasses and clovers whose seasons of growth were successional, providing continuous grazing through as long a season as possible. Hay or silage mixtures, on the other hand, try to bring everything to its maximum growth all together, for harvesting.

But first the fields had to be ploughed, so we bought a second-hand plough and a chain harrow and arranged to borrow the rest of the tackle when the time came. 'Do you know anything about ploughing?' Desmond hopefully asked Dai, who had joined us by this time. 'Fuck, no, never ploughed a furrow in my life,' replied Dai cheerfully. 'But we'll manage it somehow. I'll ask my father about it.'

So Dai asked Vic, his father, that evening, and came back with the message that as it was a grass field, it should be ploughed all in the same direction, so that the final sward would be smooth, without dips or ridges. Ploughing for corn is done in 'lands', the ploughman adding to one section as he goes to, and the other as he goes fro. While this is twice as quick, it means that where the lands meet, with their furrows falling in opposite directions, there must be either a ridge or a valley, which will still show up when the tilth is completed and the crop sown. As Vic said, 'Those old bumps are a nuisance when you're cutting over a field, and you'll have to go over it for thistles, even if it isn't a hayfield. It's worth the extra time in the beginning to do it one way and get it smooth.' He also offered to come and 'set' the plough for them if they got into any difficulties.

Many people are lyrical about the joys of ploughing, and I can quite see why, as long as I am not the one who is doing it. I have only ploughed one furrow, and the heavy tilt of the tractor, with two wheels in the furrow and two on the unploughed bit made me feel it was going to roll over any second as we lurched and jolted down the field. There was not any real danger, it was not really a very steep field, and luckily Desmond is not such a coward as I am, but I have always been right out of my element with tractors. So I was not a member of the party that set off one soft spring morning to give Cae Uchaf a face-lift. I stayed behind to finish washing the milking machines.

The boys drove the tractor to the top of the hill, dropped the hydraulics, and started cautiously down again. The ploughshares swam into the earth—the disc coulters sheared through the turf—the mould-boards swung the furrows over in that lyrical curve that so recalls the toppling of a breaking wave. They were ploughing!

Walking behind the plough you can hear the faint susurration of the metal through the earth; the friction polishes the mould-boards bright as silver. A wonderful fresh smell comes from the newly-turned furrows, and before long a tail of rooks and gulls appears, to lend authenticity to the scene.

But before the boys had completed six turns down the field, they were aware of somebody coming hastily through the gate into it. It was Vic. He stumbled up the furrow, waving his arms and shouting to them to stop. He was quite out of breath when he reached them.

'Now then,' he said. 'You're going much too fast. I could see you from over home, so I thought I'd better just jump in the car and come over to tell you before you got it all spoiled.' And he pointed out how the quickly-turned furrows were thrown too far over, and shattered, instead of lying in neat slices. Sloppy ploughing like that leaves a 'flag' of grass unburied at the lip of the furrow, which soon grows again, so your newly-sown grass is contaminated by stripes of the old weedy sward. He adjusted the plough a little too, correcting its depth and angle, and watched them each plough a few bouts before driving away, back to his own farm.

A day or two later Desmond met Howell, who said 'I saw you

43

ploughing the other day, and I shouted over the field to you to go slower, but you didn't hear me. You get too much furrow shatter if you go as fast as that. I was going to come over, but then I saw Vic there, so I knew it would be all right.' Truly, a man can have plenty of teachers, if he is willing to learn.

The field looked lovely ploughed, a warm pinky brown, and in the early mornings the furrows, which lay towards the east, were all edged with silver. Tall saplings grew in the bottom hedge, and from the cowshed you could look between the slender grey trunks at the rising swell of the fresh damp earth. But the beauty of spring ploughing is transient—you must press on. The roller flattens the furrows down, and the disc harrows, an arrangement of sharp metal wheels loose on their axles, chop them up, till the lovely striping is replaced by a soft, even tilth. You spread slag, and the field is black; lime, and it is white. Two passes with the spinner, raining down pellets of artificial fertiliser the first time and the seed itself the second time. A final harrowing and rolling —and then you wait, praying for a warm and gentle rain.

All being well, you wait for nine days, which seems a long time, and you worry. You keep going up to the field and scanning, which you do by lying down and looking flat along the ground. And then on the ninth day, you can discern as you scan, the faintest and tenderest green haze, almost like a faint bloom of algae. Get to your feet and look from that angle—it is gone. Lie down and give it the benefit of that sideways squint again—it is there! A million million thread-like grass seedlings, hardly visible against the brown matrix, have started into growth, and by the end of another week, even short-sighted Howell can stand in his yard and see if you sowed evenly, or if you left any bare patches.

We have had our moments in this matter; one field looked like a pair of striped pyjamas for years after a misjudgement of the width the spinner was casting the seed, and, like a city set on a hill, it cannot be hid. But the resultant ribbing is entirely good-natured, and you take it in good part. After all, somebody else is going to make a fool of himself one of these days, and then you can have your turn to laugh.

Of course we did not plough all the fields at once. It took us four or five years to work round the farm, and now we are re-seeding some fields for the second time. A re-seed from the previous year always starts into growth earlier in the spring than an older sward, so most dairy farmers like to plough one field a

44

year for that precious 'early bite' that stimulates the milk so well.

Dai had joined us before the bulk of the cows started to calve down in the second year, but the first one calved before his arrival, and by chance I was by myself on the farm when she went into labour. Desmond was away for the day looking at a poultry unit somewhere.

Whenever a cow is preparing to calve, the tendons of her pelvis slacken, and you can put your fist into the hollows between her tail-head and the sharp knobby pin-bones on either side of it. Dai calls this phenomenon 'shinking' which sounds funny in the past tense: 'Has she shunk yet?' Her udder rapidly enlarges and gets very firm, and her vulva becomes floppy, with trails of mucus coming from it. In a normal calving, sooner or later you see the cow straining with the rhythmic contractions of birth, and eventually a little thing like a balloon emerges. This is the bag that surrounds the calf, and within it you should be able to discern two little feet. Calving can be very quick indeed, a few minutes only, or it may take an hour or two; but when I had had Ladysmock in the calving box in labour for four hours and she still hadn't produced, I rang Mr. Harries. She kept straining away, obviously in pain, and looking round at her flanks; sometimes she stood up, and sometimes she lay down, but although occasionally the tips of a little pair of feet appeared, they kept sinking back again, and I didn't quite know what to do about it.

Mr. Harries was in, luckily, when I telephoned to describe the predicament. I told him about the feet. 'Which way up are they?' he asked. 'Soles towards the ceiling? That's a breech, then, I'll have to pull it. Time it was out after four hours. Have a bucket of warm water ready, with soap and a towel.'

When he arrived, the first thing he did, after donning a rubber overall like the A.I. man's, was to tie Ladysmock up tightly. Then he produced a couple of strong nylon cords, which he soaked in the bucket, while he soaped his right hand and arm. Plunging it into the groaning cow he felt around for a moment, and nodded in a satisfied way. 'Simple breech presentation' he said. 'We'll soon have this away. Pass me those calving ropes.' The ropes were fastened to the calf's legs, deep inside the cow, and passed round Mr. Harries' back, so that he could pull with the full strength of his body. He leaned back and heaved; Ladysmock heaved too, and bellowed; and suddenly, out shot a little

45

red heifer calf, upside down, with a flourish of little purple teats like a bunch of polyps. 'She's a bit short of oxygen' explained Mr. Harries. 'She's been in that tight birth canal for quite a long time. But she's breathing nicely now, she'll soon pink up.'

He went on to explain that a breech calf often had to be pulled, as the presenting back legs don't distend the cervix as well as the front feet and head of the normally presented calf. Then, popping a precautionary pessary into Ladysmock, who was now happily licking her calf, he jumped into his car and drove away.

In the years that followed Mr. Harries helped us with various difficult calvings, and I know of no such feeling of exquisite relief as when the vet's car drives on to the yard in such circumstances. One fine summer morning he was with us delivering an awkward calf from a narrow first-calver at the same time as the A.I. man was doing his thing to another animal. 'Why can't you put them in straight?' shouted Mr. Harries jocularly. 'Put you out of business if I did!' returned the A.I. man smartly enough.

The colour of the calf was rather a surprise. Hoping for small calves and easy calvings to compensate for our inexperience, we had inseminated the cows with semen from Aberdeen Angus bulls. This is a beef breed, but although it ends up quite hefty, it is small-boned, and tends to produce a small, neat calf. Farmers often use an Angus bull on heifers for this reason. It is a black breed, and hornless, or polled, and both these characteristics are normally passed on to the offspring. But, as we now discovered, some bulls carry a red recessive gene, and such a bull, mated with a red cow, throws a fair proportion of red calves. It was a nuisance to have a red calf, because dealers do not recognise the Angus blood that will give the calf a fair beef potential, and you get less money for it.

Several of the other calves calved normally after Ladysmock, and we soon had quite a little family of shiny black boys and girls skipping around with the one red calf in the old stable. The next unusual one was from a white cow called Mistletoe. Dai was with us by now, and when he came back from his evening visit home, he would often walk round the stock before going to bed. On this occasion we were doing the same thing, and we all met up. Walking along the edge of the Dip and looking down on the cattle peacefully grazing below, something caught Dai's eye. 'What's that by Mistletoe?' he asked. We strained our eyes through the gathering dusk at the little dark patch. What was it?

A small patch of nettles? An extra-large cowpat? Whatever it was, it didn't interest Mistletoe very much; she was grazing near it, but not paying it any attention. We scrambled down. Amazingly, it was a tiny calf. He was alive, but very weak and straggly, and unable to stand, and his mother, having licked him, had lost interest when he had failed to get to his feet and suckle. Some cows are not very maternal.

It is of the utmost importance that calves get colostrum or first milk from their mothers as soon as possible after they are born. A weak, premature calf particularly needs the resistance to infection that colostrum confers. So we set about giving this boy his dose before taking him up to the buildings for the night. Dai slipped his belt round Mistletoe's neck, like a halter, to hold her still; Desmond supported the feeble, buckling calf, and I squirted a few drops of milk into his mouth, and homed him on to the teat with my finger. It was an awkward, fiddling business, but it turned out that his sucking reflex was well developed even if his legs were out of control. Once the teat was in his mouth, he pulled at it strongly, and in about ten minutes we felt that he had had enough to see him through the night.

We released Mistletoe, who wandered away unconcernedly, a pale shape in the warm May darkness, and carried the little calf up to the buildings. When we got him into the electric light, we were surprised to see that he wasn't really black at all. Tufts of white here and there and a general sprinkling of white hairs in the black everywhere else gave him an appearance both mottled and blue. He looked like a small slice of very ripe cheese, and we christened him Stilton.

Although he grew rather slowly, Stilton survived, and became quite a character. As he was too weak at first to go in with the other calves, we made him a pen in the heifer-house hay passage, and there he spent his first few weeks. Before he learned to stand, we used to prop him up against the wall for feeding, which was quite a business. Going in with the bucket of milk, you would find him deeply asleep—really comatose, as limp as a rag doll. This frightened us at first, we thought he was dying, but by chance we read somewhere that it is normal for premature calves to become deeply unconscious, and it all became part of the routine. Putting the milk down somewhere safe but within reach, you would shake him quite hard to wake him up, and it was curious to see how his floppy limbs stiffened up as consciousness

47

came slowly back to him. When he was awake, you would haul him to a standing position, and prop him against the wall with your knee under his belly while you reached for the milk, and with your left forefinger in his mouth, encouraged him to dip his mouth into the bucket and suck.

We kept Stilton for about a year before we sold him, and he was always funny rather than beautiful. 'What are you keeping that one for? A stud bull to improve your stock?' farmer friends would say, falling around with mirth at the sight of the odd, parti-coloured little runt. But I always had a soft spot for Stilton, and he certainly never lacked self-confidence, whatever anybody else may have thought about him.

Stilton was quite quick in learning how to drink out of a bucket, without a finger in his mouth, or any other assistance, but some of the other calves were awful. It has been our experience that Aberdeen Angus calves are particularly difficult to bucket-feed, and with that batch, our expertise matched theirs.

Desmond and I were not the only ones to find them difficult. I remember passing the stable door one day and hearing desperate imprecations issuing forth in Dai's voice. 'All right! All right then! Drink or bloody drown!' Thump! Splosh! The trouble is that a calf's natural feeding position is with its head up, and of course, to drink from a bucket, it has to learn to hold it down. To start sucking, it also needs the stimulus of something in its mouth, which has to be your finger. Cows don't have top teeth in front, but they are born with a very sharp set of little bottom teeth, and an awkward feeder can make your finger quite sore. You have to bend over, too, to manoeuvre the calf's mouth into the bucket of milk, and by the time you have finished an awkward one, your back is crippled. Your patience is sorely tried too by the way some calves will repeatedly jerk their heads up and away from the milk just when you have got them drinking nicely. Putting any restraint or pressure on the back of their heads is self-defeating, because they instantly panic and begin to struggle, while all thought of drinking flies out of their minds.

Calves sucking from a cow stimulate the milk flow by giving an occasional great butt at the udder. Although the cow is sometimes nearly lifted off her feet, she usually takes it quite calmly. But when calves go through the same motions in bucket feeding, the milk is violently sloshed out of the bucket, some onto the floor, but most of all over the person doing the feeding. Drenched,

aching and sore, you tell yourself that this is not their fault—
they are simply following their instinct. If anyone is at fault, it
is you, for thwarting them. But there cannot be many people
who have dealt with a lot of calves who have not occasionally lost
their tempers. You cuff the calf—it becomes frightened—and the
problem is even more compounded. I have often come out of a
calf pen feeling thoroughly ashamed of myself for a failure in
patience. But experience worketh hope; most calves, particularly
Friesians, take to the bucket very easily, and we have had quite
a few who have managed 'without finger' from half-way through
on the very first occasion.

There are calf feeding machines which enable the animals to
suck with their heads raised in the natural position, but these are
expensive, and I have no experience of them.

Some farmers let calves stay with their own mothers for a week
or so, and then transfer them to another cow, whose sole duty is
suckling calves. There is no doubt that this is the most advan-
tageous method of rearing from the calf's point of view. But it is
hard for the mother, who has time to form a strong bond with
the calf before it is suddenly whipped away to its foster-mother.
You can often hear a bereaved cow, down the valley, mooing
after its calf night and day for as long as three days on this system, and it seemed to us not very kind, so we stuck to the bucket.

Disposing of the black calves taught us one of our earliest
lessons in looking after ourselves. Dealers often drive round farms
hoping to pick up calves on the cheap. They offer a low price,
garnished with a lot of supplementary chat. The trade is back
this week—they say. Calves five pounds less than they were a
week ago! 'Let me have him, Boss' they say. 'Think of the time
you'll be wasting taking him down to the mart. You know me'
they say, 'I wouldn't do you no wrong. I'll take him off your
hands now and save you the trouble.' And although you know
in your heart that it is all talk—that the calf trade is probably
booming, that you do indeed know him well, and that he'd
probably have the shirt off your back if he saw his way clear to
it—yet you are tempted by the trouble-saving aspect of it, and
you do sometimes give in, and sell on the yard. In the same way,
people go on making bets even though everybody knows that the
bookmaker is the only consistent winner.

So when this curly-headed little dealer jumped out of his big
car on our yard with his 'Got any calves for me today, Boss?'

we should have known, we should have sent him about his business. But we were so green. We showed him the calves, looking lovely in their clean, strawy pens. They ranged from one to three weeks old. He looked at them, and at us, and instantly realised that we were suckers. 'Bit small, they are,' he said. 'Better keep them for a week or two and get a bit of size on 'em. I'll give you a good price for them when they've grown on a bit.'

'What a kind chap,' we said, innocently, when he had gone, and continued to buy milk powder and coarse calf mixture in ever-increasing quantities.

Twice more he visited us, advising us to hold them, and the oldest were seven or eight weeks old before he said 'I'll buy those calves from you now, Boss. You take 'em down to the mart Wednesday, and I'll buy them from you in the ring. Then you can see I'll be offering you a fair price, isn't it?'

The point of these machinations was manifest to us when we got down to the market. Our calves were bigger than most of the others on offer, but less shiny, and somehow different-looking. Howell happened to be there, and he looked at them and shook his head. 'Too old now,' he said. 'They've lost their baby bloom. You want to bring them down when they're one–two weeks old. Nobody wants them at this age, they're in between, somehow.' How right he was! When the time came for our calves to go through the ring, the previously brisk trade stagnated, and they knocked down at a give-away price to guess who?

'I expect he had all the other dealers warned off,' said Desmond. 'He's probably been round saying "This is my fool—I've been nursing him along for weeks—lay off him boys!"'

So we devised a plan to try and thwart his scheming, and the following week, got somebody else to take the next three calves down and put them through the ring for us, while we lurked anonymously at the back of the crowd. But there was no improvement in the prices. 'Had any calves down here today?' asked our curly friend, after the auction was over, meeting us on the edge of the crowd. 'No,' lied Desmond, looking him frankly in the eye. 'Funny' he riposted with a sly glance. 'I thought you did. Numbers 265, 269, and 273. I bought them actually. But it's a pity you hung onto those calves so long. You'd have had better prices if you'd sent them down at one–two weeks. They lose their bloom, you know, if you keep them too long.' We were so dumbfounded by this bland bit of cheek that we forgot the mouthful we had had in store for him, and he slipped away unscathed. No doubt he had been arranging a buyer for 'six well-reared Angus calves' during the six weeks he had been advising us to hang onto them, and no doubt he rubbed his hands with glee over a handsome profit. But we learned a lesson.

Not wanting to give the remaining calves away, we decided to keep them through the winter and sell them as 'stores' the following spring, so after they were weaned, we turned them onto Llethr Ganol to grow on the grass. They proved to have a perfect genius for getting out, and trying to sort them from Elwyn's young stock and chase them back to our side of the fence was like herding the proverbial sackful of fleas.

On one occasion when they had made yet another hole in the fence (their twenty-third), Dai and I went up to get them back. After much running about we had separated and repatriated all but one. This one, the biggest, a black heifer from a big brown cow called Honeysuckle, defied all our efforts, and having chased her in vain for about twenty minutes, we decided to adopt different tactics. 'If we can get her in a corner or somewhere,' said Dai, 'I'll catch hold of her, and we can tie that bit of string from your coat round her neck. Then we'll have something to hang on to, and we'll drag the bugger back if we can't drive her.' So we cunningly manoeuvred until we had her in the angle of two hedges. But we had underestimated her passionate devotion to the cause of freedom. Seeing herself trapped, she let out a frantic bellow, and plunged between us. Dai made a despairing grab as she passed, but only succeeded in seizing her by the end of her tail. Away they went over stock and stone, like something out of Grimm's *Fairy Tales*, she bawling and bucking, he bounding after as if in seven-league boots, spectacles knocked down his nose, knitted cap on the back of his head, black tail firmly in his fist. I am afraid I quite ceased to be useful at this point, and fell around on the ground, until Dai, having broken the world sprint record by several seconds, was forced to let go.

We were finally obliged to drive the whole bunch down into Elwyn's cowshed, and sort his stock out one by one. Then we borrowed a halter, and in the confined space of the shed, managed to catch her and get it on. And that, apart from the fact that she persistently tried to hang herself all the way home, was that. But there still flashes upon my inward eye sometimes the spirited memory of Dai's chase, and I think, with Eliot, 'I should have lost a gesture and a pose.'

We never did much good with that bunch of calves, and it is not a cross I would recommend. 'Five pounds a head for your bunch of black mice,' offered a waggish neighbour, and though we did a little better than that, the experience confirmed us in our conclusion that the Ayrshire was really not the cow for the district, and that we ought to change over as soon as possible to Friesians.

FIVE

THE GREAT LEAP FORWARD

Our year of dairying had been, in spite of traumas, so agreeable and so profitable that we now decided to commit ourselves much more fully to it. We would fall in with local practice by changing from Ayrshires to Friesians, and we further aimed to raise the size of the milking herd to sixty animals. This of course necessitated a complete set of new buildings, but there was at the time a 30 per cent government grant on this kind of expenditure, and we reassured one another that our own investment would be well covered by the extra value the good buildings would add to the farm.

So we made our calculations, consulted our Advisory Officer, and went to see the Bank Manager again. The upshot of it all was that we came away with permission to borrow up to a further £6,000.

It is curious now to find ourselves on the other side of the fence, in the old codgers' camp, shaking experienced heads at the young and progressive. We were so determinedly go-ahead in those days. Circumstances alter cases, truly, and there may again come a time when agriculture can afford the expensive inputs of capital that a major re-think always needs. But we are unreservedly sorry for the second £6,000 that we borrowed, and we have seen long faces on many other dairy farmers too, who expanded their businesses on borrowed money at that time.

It seemed so easy with our one year's experience, and costings done on the back of an envelope. A cow needs roughly an acre of land to keep her for a year—half an acre for grazing, and half an acre to be conserved for winter forage, in the form of hay or silage. Her milk—1,000 gallons, say—brought you in an income of about £100. Cake, say twenty-three hundredweights, might cost about £30. Vet, A.I. depreciation, fertilisers, and a few et ceteras, would account for, say, another £25. So you would have a margin on the milk sales of about £45, to which you could add the price you got for her calf, say £20, giving you a final figure of £65. Now hay at this time could be bought easily enough at £10 a ton, and it seemed an obvious inference that an acre of land would be more profitably used to provide grazing for two cows, whose hay would be bought in, than for one, with her forage home-made.

So far so good. In theory the sum is unassailable, and there are people even now who seem to make it work in practice. Likewise, there are people who write best-sellers, climb Mount Everest, and eat twenty-five boiled eggs at one sitting. It takes a prodigious determination to do any of these things—careful planning, relentless attention to detail, and a fair measure of good luck.

In practice, a number of things can go wrong. Doubling the cow numbers doubles the number of sharp little feet cutting up your fields and gateways in wet weather—you get pasture damage, slower re-growth of grass, and a lot more foot troubles from infections passed on in the muddy sloughs. A bigger social group is more stressful for the cattle even when they are out in the fields; top-rankers have more work to keep their places in the pecking order, while lower rankers are even more hopelessly bullied.

As your main ambition in increasing your cow numbers is to swell your profits, you will not wish to throw money away on unnecessary labour, and will no doubt choose one of the more labour-saving systems. You will install loose housing, where the cleaning out can be done by a tractor and scraper rather than a shovel and wheelbarrow; you will put in a milking parlour, where the cows come to the milking machine instead of the old-fashioned bucket plant, where the machines are carried round the cows in the cowshed. You will also have to buy or rear the extra cows you need.

All this will necessarily put you in hock for a good many thousand pounds. You will need the production you hoped for from your extra cows for a good many years to pay it off. But things can go wrong. Everyone I have spoken to who has changed from a cowshed system to loose housing has found that average milk yields have dropped by up to two hundred gallons, compared with the production of the same cows tied up in a cowshed. It does not seem right; you would think that cows in cubicles, with warm, dry, beds, free to come and go as they like, to stroll out and eat a bit from the silage clamp, to drink from the trough, to turn round and lick themselves at will, would be happier and do better than tied-up cows. But of course the one element that freedom introduces is competition. A nervous cow like Comfrey or Clover is safe tied up in her stall. Her food is put in front of her—it is hers; no bullying Holly or Hawthorn can ram, blunt-headed, into her side and frighten her off. Water is available six inches in front of her nose in her own personal water bowl. She can relax, and that relaxation seems to be the difference for many cows between a daily peak of six gallons, and a really promising flood of eight or nine.

This is not to say, of course, that it is impossible to keep cows profitably on loose-housing systems; most of the cows in this country are so managed now. But it is surprising how often you find that the people who win prizes for really high-yielding herds have their cows tied up in a good old-fashioned cowshed.

The other gamble you take in a long-term investment of this kind is in the value of the various component parts. Take money itself—if you do your borrowing through the bank, you may find yourself struggling to pay back at 15 per cent money which you borrowed at 7 per cent—and the more than doubling of the interest rate alone can make your sums look pretty sick. Or hay. When we first became farmers, any dealer would sell you excel-lent hay for £10 a ton, delivered onto the farm. But this year (1975) hay prices actually touched a top price of £150 (though they came down a bit later), a price that even Grundy would find it hard to show a commercial return on.

Cattle themselves fluctuate widely in value. At Harry's sale eleven years ago, his cows averaged £120, which we thought was dear, although they were nice animals. Since then we have watched cows of a similar quality swing up to £300, and then down to about £100. Now they are on the rise again, but who dares to forecast five years ahead? We have seen the calf trade vary so that in different years £8 and £80 would have seemed a reasonable offer for the same calf. The European beef mountain had a disastrous effect on the cattle trade last autumn; people were actually giving calves away, and a friend of ours had a cheque from the auctioneers for 8p—all that was left after commission and market dues had been deducted from the sale, for 25p, of quite a nice Friesian bull calf. We told him to keep it as a sou-venir, but he said it might be more useful to give it to his M.P.

Other costs have gone up too. Cattle cake, which was about

55

£25 a ton when we started is now over £80; fertilisers too cost several times their then value. It is true that the price of milk has risen, but not proportionately. There is no doubt that dairying profits are not what they were, when we started. Labour too has priced itself out of the market for the small farmer, and many of the farms that kept a servant-boy ten years ago are now perforce managing without one.

Our experience of this sort of thing has led to a certain cynicism when we hear the politicians talking about farming. Most of the farms in this country are run far below their full productive potential for commercial reasons—simply because with the way the system is set up, intensive production, highly capitalised, does not pay. My own opinion is that if our politicians really wanted us to produce our own food rather than running an endless balance-of-payments deficit, it could quite easily be arranged. One is led to wonder if perhaps the secret price of our entry into the European community was an undertaking to play down home agriculture, to make ourselves into an outlet for the produce of the more obviously agricultural countries in the community, and to get benefits only on the industrial front. If this is not true, one wonders why there is so little inducement to produce more. On this little farm alone I am sure that we could produce four times the food we do if the end product could be sold for enough money to pay the labour it would need. But nobody is going to work as hard as that either to make a loss, or to have all their profits taken away in taxation, so the systems are run down to a comfortable jog-trot, and the ship of state wallows along through the economic storm, leaking at every joint. A nice mixed metaphor.

Let nobody think that I am advocating nationalisation of the land or state intervention beyond what we now have. Every farmer I know works twice as hard as your forty-hour a week industrial worker, and the passionate involvement of the owner is a prime necessity for any kind of farming. But what I do suggest is that carrot works better than stick, and that if the powers that be really want farmers to produce more food, as they say in their white papers, they should make it worth their while to do so.

The only way to improve your farm and raise your production without incurring a millstone of debt is to do most of the work yourself, and we have watched two or three farmers of our

56

acquaintance go through this process. My soul has fainted within me as I have watched lorry after lorry turn in at their farm gates, with sand, with chippings, with cement, with timber, with drainpipes, with concrete blocks. Over a period of five years, two farms I know have been completely modernised out of profits, without any borrowing. But the price has been that both the farmer and his wife have had to work, and work hard, from six in the morning till nine at night, six days a week—they allow themselves a little leisure between milkings on Sundays! I admire them as men of iron, but I think the price is too high. For me, time to stand and stare is as much a necessity as an early morning cup of tea. In this may perhaps be seen the decadence of the city-bred as opposed to the true countryman.

But all this is hindsight, and in our first flush of enthusiasm, we seized the bit between our teeth and galloped away in all directions. We spent money like water. Having persuaded everybody that it would be a good idea for us to go up to sixty cows, buying all their fodder, we used our new overdraft facilities and set briskly about the expansion.

The first necessity was a building to house all these new cows in. Our twenty-tie cowshed was totally inadequate, and a large building was planned, with cubicles for the cows to lie in, and a space for a new milking parlour in an extra bay at one end. Eventually we changed our minds about that, and installed a parlour in the old cowshed; but a lot of water had to flow under Meidrim bridge before that time came.

We chose the building we considered the best, albeit not the cheapest. Eighty by forty-five feet, it is a clearspan, pitched-roofed building of pre-cast concrete, substantial and permanent, and needing no upkeep. We have always found out that it lived up to what its makers said it would do; one aspect of the deal, however, caused us a wry smile or two.

As we were doing the expansion by courtesy of the bank, we arranged to pay cash for the building, a term which in those days was generally interpreted as meaning payment by the end of the month following delivery.

Delivery and erection duly followed the completion of these arrangements. Men arrived, and laid a working platform of great balks of timber, onto which a big yellow lorry carefully deposited a big yellow crane. Pausing only when the wind grew dangerously high, the crane swung the great concrete stanchions into place;

holes were dug, concrete was poured in, asbestos sheets were nailed on; incredibly quickly the thing was completed.

So far so good—we were tremendously impressed, and as the crew drove away on the Friday night, we congratulated them on a good job well done. On Monday, the bill arrived, and was tucked into the 'Unpaid Invoices' folder, to be dealt with in due course. But due course for us was not due course for them, as we discovered on Wednesday, when a further letter arrived. 'Dear Sir, We have not yet received your cheque in settlement of our invoice of the . . . th inst., and we would appreciate it if you could . . . etc. etc.' This, too, went into the folder. On Friday the telephone rang while we were having breakfast, and Desmond went to answer it. It was the Sales Manager, on long distance. He seemed puzzled, and a little pained. 'I understand that your . . . building was erected last Friday, but we still don't seem to have had your cheque. Is there anything wrong?'

What made all this so nice was the advertising slogan that the firm was running at the time. 'It's not so much the set-up, or the put-up—it's the *follow-up*!' How right they were.

Having set their anxious breasts at rest with the sum they requested, we turned our attention to augmenting the dairy herd. For our first Friesians, we went to the large dealers, Kenneth Beeston's. This was the same firm that had originally supplied us with Ayrshires, and now we ordered six freshly-calved super-quality cows, to be chosen by them, without our having seen them. And super-quality they were, too. We had plenty of grass in those days, with one or two fields already re-seeded, and cake was cheap enough to be used 'by the book'. It is not too difficult to get good production when you don't have to count the cost too much, and in the euphoria of our new big overdraft, we gave those cows everything that the bovine heart could desire.

The cubicles had not yet been installed in the new covered yard building, so the cattle were loose in there, bedded on straw, but the twenty most freshly-calved at any one time we still kept in the cowshed, tied up, warm and safe.

They were happy days as we went into the autumn, in the Year of the Great Leap Forward. Up at six, the three of us would go out to the shed to start the milking, and once it was under way, I would dart back to the house to get the early morning cup of tea. Mugs didn't last long in the cowshed, so we took to using jam-jars, and we found that the curved-in top kept the heat in

58

amazingly well, although it formed a hazard when you came to drink the last few drops. Doorsteps of fresh bread and lovely country butter, generously spread, kept the inner man going until breakfast, and twice a week, when the baker called, we varied the routine with warm, sugary doughnuts from the back of his van.

It was lovely to glance out of the open top doors of the cow-shed and see the stars paling before the morning light, and the light strengthening, and the grey hoar-frost going back across the valley. The beams of the rising sun would illumine the milk-white pine-ends of the farms on the opposite hill while the village still lay in frost and shadow; over and over again I would say to Desmond, 'Do get the camera and take a photograph of the valley. It's looking so lovely.' Poor man, he usually obliged, knowing that I can't seem to hold a camera steady at any target, and the result is that we have more photographs of 'Our Valley in the Frost' than most people have had hot dinners.

The new cows were a joy, too, standing there in line, munching their cake and milking as if they liked it. A bucket unit milking machine has a capacity of five gallons, and for eight of the cows milking then, we regularly had to change the bucket over in the course of the milking because it was full, and the milk was in danger of beginning to go up the air-pipe. Abundance is a pleasing concept even in the abstract, and the more so when it is linked to a healthy flow into your bank balance.

The only fly in the ointment was that we had more cows to milk than places in the cowshed, and when the first, most fruitful batch had been finished, they had to be turned out while the lower yielders from the covered yard were attended to. The first batch waited in the front yard meanwhile, and soon, as cows will, they made it very mucky. It was not a concrete yard, but a kind of rammed stone, and it was exceedingly hard to keep clean. The shovel on concrete flicks smoothly up with a beautiful sense of rhythm, but on a stony surface your deftness is thwarted by an irregularity—your wrist receives a nasty jar, and your shovel-ful of muck slops back onto the ground. Nobody liked cleaning the front yard, so there was a fatal tendency to leave it. We got used to wading through six inches of slurry, but every now and then we would suddenly realise how disgusting it was and have a grand clean-up. We always resolved after one of these orgies of purification to *keep* it clean and not let it accumulate again, but

59

it wasn't until the installation of the parlour, two or three years later, with proper concrete collecting and dispersal yards, that we finally got on top of the probem.

We continued to buy Friesians for a few years, both to increase our numbers and to replace the Ayrshires, most of which we sold as they calved. Several of them were bought by farmers living quite near us, and it was pleasant to look over somebody's fence and see Ladysmock or Coriander as the case might be, obviously happy and thriving.

The first Friesians we bought were ordinary commercial cattle, but knowing we were interested in pedigree, a neighbour called Sid Picton, who had a pedigree herd himself, asked us if we would like to go with him to a very splendid sale in Pembrokeshire, where the 'Entire Milking Portion' of a famous herd was being sold, as a result of the owner's ill health.

The sale was being held at Pembroke Dock, and you could see the farm element in the traffic getting more concentrated as we got nearer to our destination. Following the 'To The Sale' notices, we turned off the main road and wound our way through narrow lanes, overhung by oak trees, and stitched with the heavy white of rampion flowers, like guipure lace. We all parked, as directed, in a fine field of clover, and many a knowledgeable toe scuffed the ground approvingly as the farmers climbed out of their vehicles. 'Wish we had some of this at home' we told each other, leaving the crowded lines of Land-Rovers, Bentleys and varnished private cattle-trucks as we made our way towards the sale ring.

The ring itself, deeply littered in golden straw, had been set up alongside a Dutch barn, where more straw was stacked to make a tiered series of seats. The auctioneer's box, rather like a Punch-and-Judy theatre, was opposite. The cattle, sleek, fat and spotless, were tied in lines along the walls of the immaculate yards. Each one, groomed and polished to perfection, wore a brand new white webbing halter. Well-bred Friesians lack the wistful charm of Jerseys, but they have a stateliness of their own which always reminds me of duchesses in black satin. White-coated helpers were everywhere—one felt that the whole affair had been stage-managed with a kind of naval precision worthy of Pembroke Dock, with Orders of the Day issued: '6.15 a.m. Issue of White Halters. 6.27 a.m. Issue of White Coats. 6.31 a.m. Man the Yards!'

60

Promptly at eleven o'clock we settled, rustling, into our seats, and the auction began. The auctioneer, a nationally famous figure, extolled the virtues of the herd. He expiated on their breeding, and quoted performance statistics for several years past.

The first cow in the ring was an old one, heavy in calf, and the bidding was sluggish. 'Gentlemen! Gentlemen! What are you thinking about!' exclaimed the auctioneer, more in sorrow than in anger, like a don addressing a crowd of irresponsible undergraduates. 'A cow with this breeding is worth double this money if only for the sake of the calf she's carrying!' Eventually she was knocked down for a modest sum to a young farmer, who led her away, blushing with self-consciousness.

But his blush was as nothing compared with that of the unlucky man who accidentally moved his catalogue later on in the sale and was taken up for a bid of £1,200 guineas. 'Twelve hundred? May I say twelve? Twelve hundred I've got! Twelve hundred! Yes, you at the top there, you're in at twelve hundred!' 'I didn't bid!' cried the unhappy spectator. 'Yes, you most certainly did' replied the auctioneer firmly—and it took some impassioned pleading from the desperate farmer to save him from becoming the owner of a really expensive cow. He had to submit to quite a lecture from the auctioneer on the proper and improper use of the catalogue when a sale is in progress. 'If you insist on merely scratching your nose, as you assure me you were doing, you may not find me so lenient on another occasion.' Later on in the sale the same man actually bought a cow (on purpose this time) which I thought was extremely brave of him. I would have felt more inclined to slink away with hanging head after such a public disgrace, but he was obviously made of sterner stuff.

Later in the sale, the auctioneer could be seen to be getting tisky. He bobbed around in the box. He snorted. He made the sort of noises that are usually written down as 'Psh!' and 'Tsk!' Finally he addressed his clerk, who was standing beside him— loudly, through the microphone. 'Henry!' he said. 'Three gentlemen have elected to hold a committee meeting immediately behind this box, and I am finding it increasingly difficult to conduct the sale. Will you go and ask them to complete their business elsewhere?' Henry slipped away on this errand, but before he could reach the offenders, the irascible little man leaned right out of the box, and addressed them personally. 'Gentlemen! I trust you are well on with the agenda! This sale is perforce held up until your business is concluded!' They dispersed in haste.

The cattle at this sale were fashionably bred, as well as beautiful in themselves, and prices were high. Two animals reached £1,500 guineas, and the buyers included some of the best herds in the country. 'And she goes to Yorkshire, to the ... herd!' intoned the auctioneer, as the hammer descended, or 'Another fine animal for the ... herd in Norfolk.'

This sort of thing was beyond our reach, but we went to several humbler farm sales, buying now one, now two—even six on one occasion. It is rather amusing buying a lot of cattle at a farm sale. The auctioneer sends his clerk to take your name at the first buy, and thereafter it is part of his professional pride to recognise you. 'Cragoe, Penllwynplan' he says, as the hammer falls, and the man beside him writes it down in his book. 'Cragoe, Penllwynplan' is not one of the dealers, all of whom are well known to everybody present, and when several cows are knocked down to him, each purchase is greeted with a little buzz of interest. 'Who is he? Do you know him? Yes, he's new, English, quite mad, they say. Must have a backer. Give him six months!'

The use of good bulls through the A.I. service has enormously improved the commercial cattle in this country, and we bought some beauties for very reasonable prices. Once more we had recourse to the flower book, for the commercial Friesians were still botanical, and Nightshade, Black Bryony, Canteloupe, Black Cherries, and various others joined our herd. Very few of the cows seemed to have names, as evidenced by their A.I. certificates, which go with them if they are sold in calf, and on which they were only identified by an ear tag number. Occasionally some slight indication of personality would creep in, as with Canteloupe, on whose certificate were pencilled the words 'Cheeky white heifer'.

It was at a farm sale that we bought Candytuft, the best cow we ever had. It was quite a small dispersal, of perhaps thirty cows; we liked the look of three of them as they stood in the sheds waiting to be sold, and we were prepared to bid them up, because for once we were in the position of having some inside information!

The farmer who had done the contracting job of re-seeding our steep banks with a caterpillar tractor was quite a near neighbour of the Candytuft farm, and meeting him in the crowd before the sale began, we mentioned in conversation that there were three that we fancied. His eyes lighted up.

'Let me write them down,' he said, producing a stump of pencil from behind his ear, and a battered cigarette packet. 'And I'll see if I can find out anything about them! See you later!'

Welshmen love subtlety, and finding out things, and manipulative dealings. In a little while Ifor was back. With a conspiratorial gesture, he drew Desmond to one side and whispered in his ear. 'I've had a word with the cowman about those three cows you fancy,' he muttered, glancing warily all around, 'and he says you'll be all right! Nothing wrong with any of em! You'll be all right now!' And slipping away, he mingled with the crowd with as careful a casualness as if he had been imparting the formula for the philosopher's stone, or the details of a plot to blow up the Tower.

As it happened, the prices were not very high, and Candytuft, Lavender and Marigold became ours for not much more than a hundred pounds each. I must say they all lived up to the cowman's good word.

Another grand cow we bought was Gorse, winner of the first prize in the cow-in-milk class at the spring show and sale of commercial cattle at Carmarthen mart. A great big cow, beautifully made, she was on her way into the ring to be sold, wearing her red rosette and surrounded by a crowd of admirers and satellites who were administering last-minute dustings and polishings to her vast ebony frame. One of them turned round, and it was a man we knew. 'Do you like her?' he asked. 'It's my brother-in-law who's selling her and I know for certain she's genuine. Guaranteed! He says she'll do seven gallons, and I'll guarantee she will, I myself personally will guarantee it.'

We were so impressed with this burst of eloquence that we pursued the bidding to what seemed to us dizzy heights, and Gorse became ours at £147. She turned out to be not only as good as we had hoped, but a good deal better, on several occasions giving more than ten gallons in twenty-four hours, and finishing with a 305-day lactation of well over 1,600 gallons. When you consider that a normal standard milk churn, full to the brim, holds ten gallons, you can see what a lot it is for one cow to give in a day.

We put Gorse to a nominated bull, and she produced a heifer calf exactly like herself to look at. We reared this jewel as well

63

as we knew how, and waited with barely-controlled impatience for her to be old enough to calve. But when she did, she turned out to be one of the most useless animals we ever milked, and after three lactations of 650 to 700 gallons, we finally gave up and sent her to the barrener market.

Gorse herself came to an unhappy end too. When she was dry at the end of her second lactation with us, the time came for her to give up her place in the cowshed to a freshly-calved cow and join the common herd in the covered yard. Cattle housed on this system are not mucked out daily, but live on a rising pile of strawy dung, which is littered with dry, fresh bedding every day. Unluckily, as Gorse went into the yard for the first time, she stepped on a soft patch, and her hind feet sank in a few inches. As she stood there, looking about her, another cow, seeing a new-comer, charged her and caught her a resounding blow on the side. Her feet momentarily held, Gorse could not ride the blow by a sideways stagger, and unluckily the neck of her femur snapped under the impact. A big, heavy animal like a cow is virtually impossible to treat for a broken leg, and on the vet's recommenda-tion, we very reluctantly had to send for the knackerman. But she was a lovely cow while she lasted.

The Wednesday sale of cattle at Carmarthen is mostly com-mercial, but there is a small section devoted to pedigree stock, and it was there that we bought Bychan Prudence 63rd, a charming gentle cow who remained with us for many years and provided us with a string of pedigree heifers to register under our own prefix. This prefix, a kind of surname for your stock, is registered with the British Friesian Cattle Society, and all your cattle have it as part of their name. Ours was 'Topbush', a literal translation of the first part of our farm name. 'Pen' literally means 'head', but it is often used to mean 'top', as in 'Pen y Bryn' (top of the hill) or 'Pen y Coed' (top of the wood). 'Llwyn' means bush, tout court; nobody knows what 'plan' means, so we left that bit out.

Pedigree cattle come, of course, complete with their own names, but when we came to name their offspring, we struck out on a new line. Leaving the plant names for the non-pedigree stock, we plunged into the euphonious seas of antiquity, and came up with such stately cognomens as Topbush Atalanta, Topbush Andromeda, and Topbush Artemis. Friends criticised this as an affectation, but I always rather liked it.

Later on we ploughed two new furrows for names—birds, with Magpie, Lark, Seagull, and so on; and qualities—Prudence, Virtue, Patience, Fancy, et cetera.

The main pedigree sales in Carmarthen were held twice a year, at the market, and incorporated show classes as well. Carmarthenshire is one of the foremost dairying counties in the United Kingdom; its supporters call it 'the land of milk and money', and several nationally famous Friesian herds were near enough to send some stock and 'show the flag' as they put it, at the local fixture.

The ordinary cows for the Wednesday mart are cleaned for the occasion, but the entrants for the pedigree show and sales are scoured within an inch of their lives. For several days before the sale they are groomed, and any clotted muck is gradually soaked and brushed out of their coats. On the day of the sale itself they arrive early in the market—perhaps six o'clock—and there their toilet begins in good earnest. Some use cattle shampoos, some detergent—but most rely on a good bar of soap.

The first step is to soak the animal with warm water, thoughtfully provided by the market authorities, and work up a good lather. Rub, rub, rub, go the herdsmen, often standing one each side of the cow. Rub, rub, rub—all over, and then buckets of water are sluiced all over her to rinse it all off. Then the whole process starts again. They may make as many as four complete lathers, and the final rinse, preferably under a hose pipe, leaves her absolutely spotless. Wisps of straw and scrapers remove the worst of the wet, and a towel is produced for the white switch on the end of her tail. The rest of the tail and udder have been clipped the day before, and the tassel is now combed out with great artistry, the bigger the better. After combing, it is tied up out of the way of any possible defilement by being brought round and attached with string to the halter. The udder is bloomed over with talcum powder, the lovely clean feet are oiled, and a final pass with an oily rag gives a fine sheen to any black parts of the coat. Cows so dandied up look like new toys, freshly delivered from the shop, almost too good to be true. Funnily enough, although they get so soused with water in the process, and although most of the final rinses are cold, they never seem to take any harm from it. Less well-turned-out cows definitely do not make such good prices, unrealistic though this seems. Habitual exhibitors have a chest or trunk that they take round

65

with them with all their grooming tools in it, and inside the lid are pinned some of their rosettes and prize cards from former triumphs. Standing open in the alleyways of the mart as they dress their long-suffering charges, these chests can be quite useful as advertisements.

We bought at several of these shows and sales, and one day as we were picking our way among the paraphernalia of preparation that litters the aisles on these occasions, I was accosted by (as I thought) a perfect stranger. 'Am I mistaken?' he asked me, smiling broadly, from a great height. 'Can I possibly be mistaken?' I pointed out to him as gently as I could that without more of a lead, I couldn't tell him whether he was mistaken or not. 'Don't you know me then!' I hung my head with shame. All my life I have been bedevilled by a wretched inability to fit names to faces. Desmond often remarks that if my own father were to walk into the room unexpectedly, he'd have to introduce himself before I'd recognise him. I don't think it is quite as bad as that, but I couldn't think who this man was at all. 'It is Libby Elmer, isn't it?' (my maiden name) continued the stranger. 'Don't you remember Dolgellau?' And of course, I did, and as always I couldn't imagine how I could have failed for a moment to recognise him. It was Gwill, my farmer friend from schooldays, who used to let me ride his ponies, milk his cows (the easy ones!) and generally get underfoot to my heart's content. It was a delightful surprise to find him in Carmarthen mart buying pedigree Friesians, and by a particularly lucky dispensation of providence, he was interested in buying from a different herd from the one we were concerned with, so we spent a pleasant day sitting side by side by the auction ring and encouraging one another to spend money like water.

SIX

SILAGE

The second summer, not yet being stocked up to capacity, and hating the thought of haymaking, we decided to conserve our winter feed in the form of silage.

Silage is a form of grass conservation in which the grass is heaped up fresh, not dried, and air is excluded as far as possible. Ideally, an acid environment is built up in the clamp, and the grass is more or less pickled. If the air is not kept out, the wrong kind of acid develops, and nasty, stinking silage is the result. Good silage smells rich and edible, like plum cake sometimes, or like pipe tobacco fresh from the tin, before it is lit.

The wonder to me is that anybody ever discovered that silage was a possible result of heaping up fresh grass. Excluding the air is the factor that makes the difference between pickling and rotting, and presumably this must have been discovered by some fortunate accident rather like Charles Lamb's account of the discovery of roast pig.

Before we could start on the actual silage making, we had to prepare the silo barn, which we did with the advice and actual physical assistance of several of our neighbours. The silo barn consists of an oblong building with a barrel roof, and two filled-in sides—a long one and a short one. You make up the remaining sides with railway sleepers, standing upright side by side, and leaning back against a cross-member. The outward pressure of the tightly-packed silage holds them in place. The cross-member we got for the long side was a section of old railway line, thirty feet long. It was so heavy that I couldn't budge it an eighth of an inch as it lay on the floor, and I couldn't imagine how the boys would manage to lift it up to six feet high and strap it securely into position. But I had underestimated the enormous experience of the average working farmer in dealing with heavy things. First they strapped strong posts to the uprights of the barn, their tops exactly the right height for the cross-member. Then a tractor with a fore-end-loader was brought round, which slid under the recalcitrant steel and lifted it up like a straw with the power of its hydraulics. Balancing the thirty-foot length across the loader like an elephant balances a log on its tusks, Glyn carefully manoeuvred it into position, while everyone kept well out of the way, for there must have been the best part of a ton hanging there, and it could easily have killed anyone it dropped on—then the hydraulics were gently lowered, and the rail settled comfortably onto the tops of the posts, and rested there as if on a shelf. It was lashed with strong wire to the uprights, and remained there without a trace of shifting until we sold it some years later.

Glyn did the cutting for us, using his silerator, and his trailers. Desmond buckraked it into the clamp, and Howell, Dai, and I forked it level. Glyn drove the tractor standing up, legs widely straddled, with a fine, buccaneering air, his head adorned with a curious crimson knitted cap with a bobble on top. On closer inspection this turned out to have an unexpected hole fore and aft; it was a tea cosy. Eventually it blew back off his head and fell into the cutting flails of the silerator, which shredded it up and passed it into the trailer. Fragments of it turned up in the silage all through the winter, and were eaten by the cattle, with no ill effects.

The silage trailer tipped its loads of grass, the buckrake forked it up and backed up the ever-increasing slope with it until the wedge of consolidated grass so formed had reached the top of the short end wall, about four feet from the ground. Then there was a pause in the work, so that the remaining open end could be filled in with more sleepers. These were leaned back against a retired telegraph pole which was supported in the same way as the railway line, but which, being smaller, was simply manhandled into place.

A big ramp at the back of the silo formed the access now, and the buckraking tractor backed gingerly up with its enormous forkfuls of grass, lurching over the concrete lip of the wall and floundering across the packed grass already in there. The grass heated up quickly, and the helpers who were spreading it evenly and packing it tightly round the edges worked in a most evil atmosphere of sweating humidity. Bottles of beer were kept handily on the shelf formed by the top of the long side wall, and anyone who felt overcome could snatch some quick refreshment between the arrival of one load of grass and the next.

Every evening, after the day's work, the tractor was driven to and fro over the heap for about an hour, its big back wheels squashing the grass flat and squeezing out as much air as possible. When the silage heap gets as high as the top of the sleeper wall, this rolling can be quite dangerous. It should always be done with the tractor at an angle to the long axis of the heap; if you get a front wheel over the edge, you may live to play the violin again. Let a back wheel slip over, and you have probably had it.

Lunch was the social meal during silage-making, and Glyn was the perfect person to demonstrate the high spirits with which Welshmen divert themselves during spells of hard work. He was an inveterate practical joker, as Desmond discovered the first time he gave him a lift up the hill in the mini van. Coming up the hill from the village, it kept jumping out of gear, assisted by Glyn's discreet manipulation of the gear lever. 'I can't think what's the matter with it,' said Desmond in a puzzled voice. 'It doesn't usually do this.' 'Must be something in the water,' suggested Glyn, meeting his glance with the innocent gaze of an angel. Another of his little tricks was to stir his tea after lunch for a few minutes, and then, withdrawing the boiling hot spoon, to lay it down delicately on the back of his neighbour's hand on the table. Shrieks of one sort and another were always proceeding from Glyn's end of the table.

Glyn and Elwyn are cousins, and as they often work together, they have developed a tradition of playing tricks on one another. Some are simple enough—a little noise, when somebody is leaning forward at strain to lift a heavy bale—but laughter never comes amiss when the work is hard, and the bales do get heavy when you reach the thousandth.

One Christmas, the cousins were up at Glyn's farm, feathering Christmas poultry. Glyn, coming into the kitchen from outside, had, according to custom, taken off his gumboots and left them outside the door. Elwyn, who was 'drawing' the poultry, privily deposited therein the entire bowels of a goose, and with silent glee, awaited the shrieks of rage that he thought would be forthcoming. But on this occasion Glyn had the last word, because he did—absolutely nothing. 'There were two more days feathering before we finished' said Elwyn, 'and I was on my toes every second expecting him to catch me. But the bugger of it was that in the end he didn't do anything at all. But I know I'll have it with him one day. Just when I don't expect it!'

When most of the silage is in the clamp, you have to go more slowly, adding grass as the heap sinks, until eventually either you have finished the grass you have to cut, or the heap is full, and the shrinkage complete. Noxious black juice seeps from the bottom of a heap of making silage, which is called silage effluent, and is intensely poisonous to fish. Woe betide the farmer who allows any of this to get into a waterway. You have to be a big corporation to pollute a river and get away with it nowadays. Many farmers have been heavily fined for not making a safe soakaway for silage effluent. Luckily for us, our silage seeped very little, and what few gallons there were, disappeared into the ground within a yard of the silo, a good quarter of a mile from any stream.

To finish off your heap you can roll some trash on top, or lay a plastic sheet on to exclude air. Many farmers lay a few layers of hay or straw bales on top of the sheet to keep it firmly pressed down, but I know of at least one instance when the warmth and moisture of the silage generated spontaneous combustion in the hay, and a nasty fire was the result.

Cattle in loose housing systems usually self-feed silage over some kind of movable barrier which is kept at the right distance from the silage face. But needing to ration our silage rather tightly, we did it the hard way, cutting it out, and carrying each cow's helping to her in the cowshed or covered yard in a chaff sheet. A silage knife has a flat step thing so that you can stamp it into the consolidated material, and you cut along a strip first. Then you fork it out, and it comes away in big wads, strata, as it were, of a pleasant greeny-gold colour, and hopefully, of a wholesome smell. The cut edge had the neat, stubbly, bristly look of an old-fashioned haystack, cut with a hayknife. Not all cows are familiar with silage, and at first some of them clearly didn't realise that it was food. 'Can you eat it? Can you wear it?' one imagined them asking their neighbours in the cowshed. But within a couple of days, even the faddiest had sampled it, and decided that it was good.

Not having made enough silage for all our stock's requirements, we also bought some hay from a dealer, and the routine was to give them their silage in the morning, and their hay at night. The smell of silage, even good silage, is very penetrating, and can

70

taint milk if milk is exposed to it, so the silage feed was given after breakfast, when the milk was safely down on the churn stand. By the time evening milking came round it had all been eaten up, and the cows were finally tucked up for the night with straw bedding, and a good feed of hay last thing.

Cows can be very stupid, and the most bizarre accidents sometimes happen in a cowshed. One cow we had, Werndale Prunella, nicknamed 'Stuggy Prue' on account of her portly figure, once jumped over the bars in front of her stall and landed in the hay passage, still tied up by her neck-chain! One back leg was twined perilously among the galvanised iron bars that formed the front of the stall, and our hearts were in our mouths as we helped her out of her awkward predicament. Bent bars remained in that place to remind us of a narrow escape.

An even narrower escape befell a black cow called Trefoil, purchased at a farm sale held in the pouring rain on a nearly vertical slate farmyard up in the Bundu country. We were finishing breakfast one morning, and Dai had gone out a bit ahead of us. Suddenly he rushed back into the room, shouting 'Trefoil's back in the dunging channel strangling on her neck-chain! She's nearly gone!'

We raced to the cowshed. It was true. For some reason Trefoil had lain down a foot or eighteen inches further back than usual—perhaps she had slipped—and feeling the chain pressing awkwardly on her neck, seemed to have resigned herself to a choking death without a sign of a struggle. With all her eleven hundredweights dragging on the chain, there wasn't a chance of undoing it in the normal way, and she was too nearly unconscious to be prodded to her feet. There was nothing to do but to get the hacksaw and saw through the bolts that held the slider, on which the neckchain ran, to the stall partition. Released, Trefoil opened her eyes, grunted a couple of times—then lurched to her feet, and began to chew the cud as if nothing had happened. 'All this fuss about nothing' she seemed to be saying. Ungrateful beast!

Winter evenings, when the cows are warmly housed and fed, and work is over for the day, are great times for 'neighbouring'. Somebody who is driving past thinks to himself 'I'll just drop in and ask Cragoe if he can spare me a couple of dozen hens', or something of that sort, and once in the warm kitchen, the whisky bottle is produced, and under the benign amber influence, the stories begin to flow. The Welsh are great raconteurs; they enjoy

71

drama, and give full value to the relating of even the smallest incident.

Elwyn was with us one evening, and he was telling us how he had recently bought a fertiliser spreader from a local implement dealer, a notoriously tight man. 'I asked him for a discount, naturally,' said Elwyn, 'but no good. He wouldn't budge an inch. So after a while I came up a bit in what I was offering. But still no good—he wouldn't meet me at all. But I actually had the money with me, in notes, so then I said to him "All right man, ... pounds, and that's my last offer." And I just let him see the edge of the notes. And when he saw it was cash I was offering, he GRABBED the money and STUFFED it in his h'ass pocket. . . .' Accompanied by flashing eyes, and a wealth of pantomime gesture.

Dai was in the kitchen once when I was retailing this incident to somebody, and afterwards he took me on one side. 'Before you tell that story to anyone else, Missis,' he said, 'I think there's something I ought to tell you. Round here we more pronounce that word H'ARRRSE.'

Another of Elwyn's stories was about a certain Davies who had a bull. 'A real nasty bull it was, a proper bugger of a bull.' And one day when Davies was coming out of the bull pen, the bull charged him, and caught his finger against the gate. 'He felt it knock him boom! and when he looked at his finger, it wasn't there. The bull had knocked it clean off. So he went down to the hospital, and the doctor said "Where is the finger, Mr. Davies? Perhaps we can sew it back on." "Oh, I left it back at the farm," he said. "Whereabouts is it? Could somebody go back for it?" "Not worth it, surely," says Davies. "The cat'll have had it by now!" '

After this experience, Davies decided to sell his bull, and it was entered for the monthly auction in Carmarthen mart. But as the lorry-driver who took it was unloading it in the market, it broke away from him, and ran amok through all the scenes of early morning bustle.

'It was the lorry-driver's fault,' said Elwyn. 'He was useless—useless! Frightened of him, he was. He just went and hid under the ramp of the lorry, and Davies couldn't do much, his hand was still bad with him. And the bull was running around with his tongue sticking out, roaring, and pawing up the ground, and everybody running like hell. And in the end it took five farmers and two lorry-drivers to get him, and they got a rope over his horns, and got him that way. And he was mad! They had to put two halters on him, as well as his nose chain, and tie a sack over his eyes before they could do anything with him. And it took three men to take him into the ring, and he was roaring, and grumbling, and froth all over the place.

'The auctioneer turned his microphone up to its loudest to be heard over the noise the bull was making, and began to tell the assembled buyers what a marvellous animal it was. Its breeding— its dam's yields; its unselected daughters' average yields; the prizes it had won. Eventually he came to the end of his spiel, and turned to Mr. Davies, who was standing beside him. "Is there anything else you want to say about him. Mr. Davies?" And Davies leans over and grabs the microphone and shouts right in it. "Yes!" he says, "He's qui-et!" '

Any anecdote in Wales is apt to be interrupted at an early stage that puts the *dramatis personae* in context, a practice known to us as 'That's who he is.' 'There was a man living in Llangendeirne a few years back,' begins the narrator, 'and he bought an old Dai Brown tractor at a farm sale. That's who he is—you know that old man with a beard who's selling cabbages just inside the gate of the market? Well, his aunty is living in Gellywen, down by the bridge there, and her boy from her first husband married this chap's daughter, they were speaking to you the other day at Tom's sale, do you remember?' And then the anecdote continues, which is fine if you can still remember the beginning of it.

A steady course of 'That's who he is' over the years does fill you in eventually on the complex web of relationships, and prevents the frightful *faux pas* you can make in your ignorance. A great pitfall is the fact that most people are known only by their Christian name and the name of their farm. Desmond expressed himself freely to an acquaintance once on the subject of another farmer. 'I suppose he's rather pathetic, really,' he said, 'but I haven't much time for him, I must say. You never see him anything but drunk; he's just a sot, and if he has any redeeming features, I haven't seen them.' The man he was talking to agreed wholeheartedly enough, but Desmond was rather confounded when he discovered by chance a few days later that the two men were brothers. 'No need to worry, though,' said his informant. 'They've been bad friends for years. You couldn't say anything so

73

bad about one that the other wouldn't say anything worse.' But it taught us to be a bit more careful, and not to open our mouths too widely.

If people are not known by their farm names, as Elwyn Lan, Glyn Sarnau, Dai Oernant, they may be called after their occupation like Donald y Rhefel (the blacksmith), or Wyn Shop. Sometimes a nickname is introduced, as in Dai Trots, who does the commentaries for the trotting races, or Gwyn Moustache, who is the owner of a famous ornament. Or a notable incident may be commemorated. Once a certain local surveyor, who up to that time had been known naturally enough, as Dai Surveyor, went on a salmon poaching foray with two friends. The bailiffs surprised them, and they had to run for their lives. Taking advantage of natural cover, they fled to the farm of a friend who lived close by; he hastily bundled them into an occupied pigsty, and fended off the pursuing water bailiffs with the story that the sow in there was in the very act of producing a litter, and would certainly savage her piglets if they went poking in searching for 'these so-called imaginary poachers of yours'. Thwarted, the bailiffs withdrew, to be followed, when darkness had fallen, by their relieved quarry. But the story got around, and when by a sad chance two of the poachers died of heart attacks within the next month, some wag dubbed the third with the name he has carried ever since—Dai Survivor.

SEVEN

THE HENS

I tend to dwell on the cows, because they are what my idea of farming really is; but a much more important factor is our economy, which from the very beginning, has been the hens.

When we first decided to go into farming we realised that a small farm could only provide the sort of income we wanted if it contained an intensive (ie. non-land-using) enterprise. Of the various possibilities—pigs, broilers, turkeys, rabbits, laying hens —we chose the last, and, unexciting as it is, it has provided our bread and butter ever since.

We chose a battery system made by a firm called Grossmith, with what are quaintly named semi-colony cages. This means that the hens are caged in groups of eight or so, with a little more room to walk about than in single bird cages; the advantage from our point of view was that semi-colony cages work out cheaper per bird housed than singles.

The morality of intensive farming is a matter that my conscience is still not entirely easy about. On the one hand, there is no doubt that the battery bird is protected from virtually all of life's disagreeable elements. She lives in a controlled environment, with the temperature maintained as near 70° F as possible, and with a constant flow of fresh air from the forced ventilation. A perfectly balanced diet is in front of her almost all the time. (The trough should be clear before the next feeding time comes round, so there may be an hour or two in the twenty-four without food.) Fresh water is always available to her from the nipple-drinkers. She has room in her cage to stretch, flap her wings, and walk a few paces in either direction. Usually cage-reared from a tender age, she knows of no other environment, and as for boredom—is it possible for a creature with as tiny a brain as a hen to be bored? Commercially, it is almost a necessity to keep hens in batteries. There is no doubt that they lay more and larger eggs than free-range birds, they eat less, and costs are cut, too, by the tremendous economy of labour that the system provides.

I have seen television programmes against the battery system in which people have thrown grave doubts on the health of the birds, implying that eggs produced from such birds contained some hazard to human health. An almost naked hen was produced as evidence of this ovine ill-health, and given much sympathy as a victim of the system. It was 'very bad', averred the woman who was being interviewed, but she *might* be able to 'nurse it back to health'. As far as I could see, the only thing the matter with the hen was that it was in deep moult! It sat in its basket in front of the television cameras looking this way and that with bright eyes, making the soft interrogative clucking noises that poultry-keepers call 'talking', characteristic of the normal, healthy bird. I wouldn't have minded betting that if that hen had been put back in its cage and fed its proper ration, in a month or six weeks it would have grown a complete set of feathers, and looked as good as new. Hens in the warm atmosphere of a shed do seem to moult more completely than outdoor birds, but the temperate climate in there keeps them from apparent suffering until their feathers have grown again.

A spell in the batteries certainly does not impair the health of the average bird, as we have often proved. After a year of lay, we usually offer our birds for sale, and we have had many reports of longevity and excellent production. There is no doubt that a freer system acts as a tonic; pepped up by it, many of them go on for as long as four or five years, which is not a bad life-span for any hen. Of course, hens kept thus, domestically, are not subject to any system of costings. In business terms, they are probably not economic beyond the second year. In the batteries, we only keep them through one laying season, as shell quality tends to deteriorate after that.

Struggling to be objective and not anthropomorphic, the mind thus gives a doubtful assent to intensive poultry keeping. And yet ... and yet ... when I compare the lot of the hens in the shed with that of the few who scratch round the yard, I sometimes wonder if we have sold our souls to Mammon. Caged hens are thwarted of so many of their instincts. They cannot scratch for food—though you sometimes see them give an automatic rake at the cage floor as they eat from the trough; they cannot go into the privacy of a dark nest to lay their eggs. Broodiness is no

76

problem, because it has been bred out of them; but the instinct for flight of the lowest hen in the pecking order is thwarted too, and they are necessarily deprived of the luxury of a sunwarmed dust-bath in the busy, cluck-happy farmyard.

Not everything that comes from a farmyard is good, of course, and by being kept away from their own droppings the caged poultry are totally free from coccidiosis and 'gapes'. This distressing affliction used to bother the chickens of my childhood, which scratched on dungheaps; every now and then they would stand still with necks stretched out and mouths wide and go through a dreadful pantomime of retching. The cause, I believe, is a parasitic throatworm, and it can be fatal.

I balance the arguments, pro and con, in my mind, and it seems just about all right, but then I wonder if the factory owners of the industrial revolution went through the same process apropos of the children they so callously utilised in the course of profit. We look back with horror on many of our forbears and say to ourselves, 'How *could* they?' I wonder if our descendants will say that about our battery poultry? At any rate, we have decided that as soon as we can afford to, we shall either go out of poultry altogether, or turn to some more extensive system, such as movable arks, cutting down the numbers at the same time.

For some reason, public indignation is confined to the keeping of hens in batteries; other animals kept, for less good reasons, in close confinement, do not stir the same angry sympathy. The goldfish in its tiny bowl, the budgerigar never let out of its cage 'because he's so hard to catch again', the white mouse in its little box—even the dog, tied to the kennel for long periods and only exercised, inadequately, on the lead—do not raise the public blood-pressure at all. Hens in cages are at least regularly inspected by the Ministry of Agriculture to see that they are not overcrowded; other animals, whose sole purpose is to minister to people's selfish pleasure, are not.

Our hen-shed was erected in double-quick time by a team of men working on piecework rates, who slept in the hay-barn to save their lodging allowance, and hammered away at the job from first light in the morning until it was too dark to see. Neighbours and people from the village eyed it cautiously; nothing like this had ever been seen in Meidrim before. 'That's a grand shed,' they said, before the cages went in. 'What you going to use it for, then? Rearing calves, maybe?'

77

There was a curious reluctance to admit that poultry might be a profitable speculation. When we were still looking for a farm, Desmond had an exploratory interview with the manager of the Carmarthen branch of our bank—a person, we felt, who might become exceedingly important to us. He told him of our plans, but was firmly set right, from the very beginning, on the hen question. 'It's no good thinking about poultry in Carmarthenshire,' said the Bank Manager. 'Poultry don't *do* in Carmarthenshire, and that's a fact.' Desmond pointed out gently that the poultry we were thinking about would be in a controlled environment shed, which should presumably, if functioning properly, provide the same conditions wherever it was erected, from Chipping Sodbury to the Andes. But the Bank Manager was adamant. 'I've seen a lot of young people going into farming,' he declared, 'and many of them have made the same mistake as you. Carmarthenshire is not suited to poultry farming; they've just lost their money, and so would you, if you were to go in for it here.' Further argument being obviously pointless, we discreetly withdrew, but we did take the precaution of leaving our bank account where it was for some years instead of transferring it down here. A bank manager sympathetic to your projects is of the first importance when you are starting farming.

The first hens arrived on my birthday, 23 July, 4,000 of them, in crates, piled high on a lorry. They were white ones, laying white eggs, eighteen weeks old, and even to our inexperienced eyes they did not look a good batch.

To begin with, there was a lot of variation in size. A well-reared flock of birds should be as like peas in a pod at housing; the rearer will have handled them all several times in the course of giving them their various injections, and any obviously unthrifty little ones should have been culled out along the line. Adequate provision of space at the feeders should give every normal bird a chance to develop to its full physical potential, and a weight variation of as little as, say, ± 5 per cent should be the result.

Secondly, the birds had damaged one another in the crates. Perhaps they had been packed too closely, or stressed by being roughly handled in the catching. Whatever the reason, the results were all too horrifyingly apparent; they had been pecking one another on the journey, and sixty of them were so badly damaged that they had to be killed.

Cannibalism in white birds can be quite a problem. Motivated

78

by instinct only, the bead-brained chicken pecks inquisitively at anything bright, from a grain of barley lying on the ground to a drop of red blood on a companion's white feathers. Any trifling injury is thus quickly magnified, and a bird can be pecked to death if it is not rescued in time.

We used to treat any birds we found with wounds by brushing on a good helping of Stockholm tar. The sticky black mess discouraged pecking and concealed the bloodstained area, as well as providing an antiseptic dressing for the wound itself. Badly hurt birds were isolated until they recovered and feathered up again. Keeping the lights dim in the shed and using amber bulbs were good policies, but it continued to be somewhat of a problem until we changed from white to brown hens. The brown bird is in every way more placid than the white, and of course has the advantage that blood would not show up on it anyway. Whatever the reason, I am happy to say that pecking is now a thing of the past in our shed.

Caging birds is one of the farming jobs that I most bitterly dislike. One man stands on the lorry, catching the birds in handfuls by their legs out of the crates. Young birds are light, so they come to no harm being carried a short way by their legs, although I can't imagine it is very pleasant for them. This man hands you a cageful—say four in each hand—and away you trot down the shed to the person who is caging, who takes them from you one at a time and pushes them under the swing fronts of the cages. At first they seem light, but a shed of 4,000 takes a long time to fill, and your arms come to ache long before the end. You have to carry them with your elbows slightly bent, to prevent their heads brushing along the floor—and their hard legs, always bearing on the same part of your hands, raise blisters which are very sore. The only bonus is the fresh scent of camomile which grows round the hen-shed door. It gets very trampled on hen-putting-in days, and its spicy, appley fragrance makes a delicious contrast with the stern disinfectant smell of the newly-cleaned shed.

Perhaps I should add that we have never again had a batch of birds like the first one. We buy all our hens from a local rearer now, and they come out of the crates with hardly a feather out of place. We also know enough now to have feed ready in the troughs for new birds, so that when they are in, the job is finished. But with the first batch, we left the feeding till the end,

and as our feeding trolley hadn't arrived, we had to do it as best
we could, direct from the half-hundredweight bags. It was half
past two in the morning before we finally got to bed; I remember
remarking to Desmond that I'd never had so many waking hours
of any birthday before in my life.

The hens settled in well, and looking after them became part
of our routine. They come into lay at about twenty-two weeks
of age, and we waited eagerly for the first egg. It was tiny, of
course—pullets always start with footling little efforts that look
as if they ought to have a big red 'L' on them—but it was Production, and after feeding them for a month with no return, we
were glad to see it.

We had arranged with the local packing station to take our
eggs, and they provided us with packing material, and collected
the eggs from us in a lorry once a week. Eggs laid in battery cages
roll forward to a tray in front of the birds, where they cannot be
pecked at or trodden on, and you collect them from there direct
into Keyes trays. The design of the Keyes tray is brilliantly
simple in that the little pimply bits that keep the eggs apart nick
together when stacked, and take all the weight—the eggs are
loose in their compartments, and under no strain at all.

Collecting the eggs was a job that gave you the same lavish
feeling as pouring milk into the churns. Going into the long, dim
shed, the pale eggs would gleam, abundant, like a field of mush-
rooms. The five big fans in the roof hummed, the birds clucked
and chatted, and the big instrument panel gave it all an important
look, like a nerve-centre, the control room of an ocean liner,
perhaps, or a transatlantic jet.

Lay in hens is described in terms of a percentage of hens
housed, and 90 per cent of 4,000 birds means 3,600 eggs to pick
up every day. The packing station knocked money off for any
dirty eggs, so we had to sort through and clean them before they
were taken away. We had read that you weren't allowed to wash
eggs, so for years we scrubbed away at them with silly little hand-
sanding devices—a total waste of time, as it afterwards transpired.
We used to bring the collected eggs round to the kitchen and
stack them in their wooden travelling boxes against the wall until
we could find time to deal with them. At the rate of ten or more
cases a day, very little distraction—a burst of field work, cattle
getting out, a difficult calving—meant that we fell behind with
the job and sometimes we could hardly get into the kitchen

because of the stacks of waiting boxes. We often had to work late the day before the lorry came, but we were faithful about the freshness of our eggs and never kept any back.

As jobs go, it was not unpleasant, and we would often do it sitting in the sunshine outside the back door, chatting sociably. Visiting friends and relations who came to see how we were managing were often pressed into service on this task too, particularly when we had accumulated a bit of a backlog.

In the end we did what we should have done at the beginning, and bought an egg washing machine. Metal baskets of dirty eggs were lowered into it, and swished to and fro in warm water by its reciprocating action. It had a very characteristic little squeak, and I could never decide whether what it kept chanting was 'pig in the middle! pig in the middle!' or 'officer Dibble! officer Dibble!' At any rate, it seemed to enjoy its work, and when we discovered that a mixture of Vim and Omo worked just as well as expensive proprietary liquids, and that baskets of washed eggs dried splendidly in the forced draught of the ventilation shafts, we were away.

Our relations in general, though encouraging, found it hard to believe in our status as actual farmers. 'On a *real farm* I understand that they do it this way,' they sometimes incautiously said, and offered us titbits of information from the Archers, which they assured us was very authentic.

On one occasion my mother-in-law and one of my aunts happened to be visiting at the same time. They wanted to see the milking, so after we had tied the cows up, we fetched out two kitchen chairs for them, on which they sat talking while we moved the units from one cow to another down the line. Soon a cow, as cows will, raised her tail and splattered into the dunging channel. Our visitors looked at it with anger and disbelief. Finally, 'Dirty beast!' said my aunt with withering scorn, and with one accord they rose, seized their chairs, and departed, to continue their conversation elsewhere.

The first time we had to kill a hen was rather a shambles. It was obviously an ailing bird which needed putting away, and, having seen it done many times by experts, Desmond prepared to wring its neck. It looks so very easy to do this, and once you know how, I believe it is. (I confess with shame that after a few abortive efforts, I have given up trying.) Desmond picked up the bird, in the approved way, but in his effort to do it quickly he applied too much force, and pulled the poor thing's head right off. In horror and revulsion he flung the decapitated body to the floor of the hen-shed whereupon it leapt to its feet and rushed under the cages, where it performed a revolting *danse macabre*, with a little stalk-like bit of spine sticking out from where its head had been.

Eggs are, of course, delicate things, and accident-prone in consequence. One of my Great First Times was when I realised that the bottom tray in a stack of six I was holding was collapsing through my fingers and that there was absolutely nothing I could do about it. There wasn't even time to dump it on the ground— I just had to stand there and let 180 eggs trickle through my fingers and shatter on the floor. As well as being expensive, an accident with eggs is so disgusting to clear up, particularly as you feel in duty bound to sort through the wreckage for any survivors, to mitigate the financial loss.

My six-tray accident paled into insignificance, though, in comparison with Desmond's Homeric egg disaster. He had put six cases of eggs into the mini van to bring them round to the house for cleaning. For some reason or other they were not in wooden boxes, but just in Keyes trays, stacked ten or twelve high. Driving slowly and cautiously over the bumpy ground from the hen-house round the back of the cowshed, Desmond accelerated a fraction too much and was all of a sudden aware of a sickening lurch behind him. He drew up at once, but it was too late, the balance was destroyed and with the stately inevitability of a dynamited mill chimney, the eggs fell forward. Down his neck, in his ears, on his hair—over the passenger seat—round the pedals—rolled the eggs, while Desmond sat in despair, and previously undreamt-of oaths flew unchecked from his lips. When movement had subsided, he started up again, and drove stickily round to the front yard to begin the grand cleaning-up. The first person he met round there was the Esso representative, who had come to see him on some question about a delivery of diesel oil for the tractor. 'Don't come near me,' roared Desmond out of his wet yellow vehicle, 'I'm not responsible for my actions at the moment—I've just broken about a thousand dozen eggs.' But Tom Esso, as everyone calls him, is not a man easily daunted. With a stream of soothing noises he extricated the meringue-coated unfortunate from his nest of custard, and then very kindly stayed and helped to swill the debris out of the van.

By chance, Tom was there on another occasion when we had an accident, and again we received help and counsel from his calm, unflappable nature. We were milking this time, and the children were playing in the meal-room where the cake is stored, which opens off the cowshed. We nearly always had them in there, safely under our eye, while we milked, but on this occasion Matthew, aged four, had wandered out into the cowshed. For some reason, against standing orders, he decided to walk between the cows and through the little gate that led into the hay passage in front of them. Now the cow on the left of the little gate was Hawthorn, a nasty old besom if ever there was one, and I had the shock of my life when I looked up and saw this little creature strolling so casually along her flank. 'Matthew!' I cried. 'Come back at once!' and as he turned at the sound of my voice, Hawthorn lashed out. She caught him on the back of the head and hit him so hard that he sailed through the air, and crashed against the wall at the back of the cowshed. Had he not turned, the blow would have caught him full in the face. As it was, blood streamed from his head and screams from his mouth, and it was to this scene of carnage that Tom Esso entered. At once he summed up the situation. 'You take him to the doctor,' he told Desmond. 'He's going to need stitches for that cut. You finish the milking missis—I'd do it for you, but I don't know how. And I'll stop here and keep this little one amused, so she doesn't get into any mischief while her brother's not here.' And so he did, remaining with Rachel, who was always happy to play with him, until the milking was finished, and Desmond had returned with Matthew, and the good news that although he had had two stitches, he hadn't cried at all as they had been put in.

One day, as I was collecting eggs in the hen-shed, I noticed something that struck me as curious. The sawed-off ends of the cage-frames looked, here and there, as though they had been set with tiny garnets. Closer inspection showed that the garnets were alive, and were present, patchily, throughout the shed. Dredging about in our subconscious, the words 'red mite' floated up, and in some dismay we telephoned the Poultry Advisory Officer and asked her to come round.

She came at once, and as she told us later, her heart sank when she saw the size of our problem. Red mite is one of the most tiresome of poultry parasites, and is particularly prevalent when birds are kept intensively. The mites do not live on the birds, but

83

in crevices of the cage and building, and they make a nightly foray to the sleeping poultry to feed. The resultant irritation and loss of blood can make a substantial difference to the condition of the hens, and, consequently, to their lay. In suitable conditions—warm, and well-fed—all kinds of mites multiply prodigiously, and the red ones are no exception.

Various sprays are used for their destruction, and various spray-guns to apply the sprays. But we settled for the simplest and cheapest—a garden syringe, and a Boots product called Sebbyn. A tinful, costing only 12s. 6d., was sufficient to do the whole shed, it did no harm to the birds, and the following morning the droppings boards looked as if they had been liberally sprinkled with black pepper, with the myriad darkening bodies of the slain. A further spraying some ten days later polished off the next generation as it emerged from the egg, and we considered ourselves lucky to have controlled it all so easily. It is true that we still have to spray two or three times a year, but we have heard of people who have found the problem so intractable that they have had to give up keeping poultry because of it.

When a batch of hens comes to the end of its useful life, we put an advertisement in the papers, and people come to buy small numbers of birds, either for laying or for dressing and putting into the deep freeze. Lots of people come every year, and we enjoy seeing them, and having an annual chat. But some can be trying.

We were up on the bank one Sunday afternoon mending a fence when we saw an old man standing down by the hen-shed. He was shouting and gesticulating so wildly that we wondered if he was in some kind of trouble, and rushed down to help him. It turned out that he wanted six hens, but before we got down to business, he decided to give us a history lesson. After commenting on the view down the valley, he asked us if we had ever wondered why the fields were so small in this part of the world. Without waiting for a reply, he proceeded with the lecture he was obviously dying to give us. 'To understand the answer to this question,' he declaimed 'we have to go way back in history. Two hundred and fifty—even three hundred years ago! To the time of the Romans!' I can't remember why the Romans, presumably enjoying the neo-classicism of the early eighteenth century, had had such an influence on local topography, but I do remember that when after half an hour of potted history he went into the hen-shed, he insisted on choosing his own birds, told us that we were cruel to keep them in cages, and then tried to haggle about the price!

When all the hens have been sold, the hen-shed has to be thoroughly cleaned and disinfected. Muck is shovelled out once a week throughout the year, but cobwebs proliferate, and dust from the feed clings to them, so by the time of the Big Clean-Up, the aisles are hung with ghostly draperies, and the shed looks like Santa's Grotto in a department store at Christmas. Every inch of wall, ceiling, beam, and cage has to be brushed, washed, scrubbed and finally disinfected before a new batch of birds is put in. The feed troughs have to be dismantled and carried outside, where they are painstakingly scraped free of any hardened particles of old food, and scrubbed out. Every part of this job is hateful; the dusty part gives you hay fever, the wet part gives you chapped arms, and woe betide you if you get touched by the disinfectant. Desmond was careless once in the final spraying of the shed, and some disinfectant ran up his arms. They may have been germ-free afterwards, but they were certainly sore—the disinfectant started up an irritation which took about a fortnight to clear up.

EIGHT

THE MARKET

While the Egg Marketing Board existed, selling your eggs was as automatic as selling milk. You registered with a packer, and he was obliged to take your whole production, and pay you with due deductions for seconds and rejects, at regionally settled prices that neither he nor you had any hand in fixing. The profits on a reasonably-managed flock were modest, but secure, and the whole business was entirely trouble-free. We kept white birds, because they lay more eggs than brown ones, and plodded along in a routine sort of way from year to year with our one shed.

When the Egg Marketing Board began to totter, Desmond looked into the future and much disliked what he saw. 'Packers will be in a perfect position to put the boot in as hard as they like,' he said. 'Profitability will probably become very cyclical, as it is with pigs, and the packers will make sure that whoever's margin gets squeezed, it won't be theirs. We may find ourselves having to do our own marketing, and if we do, we won't want to get stuck with a whole load of white eggs, which nobody likes. Next time we re-stock the shed, I'm going to hedge the bet by putting in half brown birds; it'll give us more flexibility if the crunch comes.' It was lucky that he was so far-sighted.

In the October of that year when our new two-colour flock was just coming into lay, egg prices slumped. It was still in the time of the old money, and the price we were being offered by the packer averaged 10d. a dozen for our white eggs. Brown eggs had a bonus of 2d. on them, but even this left them far below the cost of production. Shop prices showed that both the packer and the retailer were taking their full 5d. margin; it was the producer who was bearing the full burden of the uncertain market, which did not seem fair. So, remembering the motto 'If you can't beat 'em, join 'em', and not being bound to our packer by any contract at this stage, we began to sell our brown eggs at the door.

We were always being asked for eggs, but when we had a
86

contract with the packer, and he was playing square with us, we had always honourably refused. Now, feeling ourselves exploited, we let the word trickle around that we had brown eggs for sale, and soon had quite a nice little business with various small shop-keepers and roundsmen. Christmas was approaching, and demand was quite brisk. But Nemesis was just around the corner.

We had hardly expected the packer to be pleased at our show of independence, but his letter still came as something of a shock. Waiting till the middle of January, when the egg business hits its yearly low point, and arranging for the letter to reach us on the day before his usual weekly collection of our eggs, he wrote to us in reproachful strain. It had come to his notice some time ago, he said, that we were selling some of our eggs privately. For months he had held his hand, hoping that this magnanimity would prick our conscience and recall us to a proper sense of duty. But seeing us apparently hardened in villainy, he had, albeit reluctantly, to let us feel the full consequence of our infidelity; in short, as of now, we could consider ourselves out on our ear.

This put us in something of a predicament. A week's white eggs were piled up in the shed, and the trade was poor. An instant conference was called round the breakfast table, and various plans were propounded. The most feasible—that Desmond should load up the van and try selling eggs at cut prices round various shops in Carmarthen—was under discussion, when the door opened, and Mike, a farmer friend from across the valley, walked in.

'Why are you looking so solemn?' he asked. We told him. 'Why don't you load up the van and take some eggs down to the market?' he asked. 'After all, that's what markets are supposed to be for, isn't it? For farmers to sell produce in, I mean. I'll come with you—it might be rather fun. Market-day's Wednesday, isn't it? The day after tomorrow? What the hell, let's have a go!'

So, as it seemed better than any of the other prospects, we decided to try it. Desmond and Mike loaded the van with 150 dozen white eggs and sallied forth into the unknown, while I waited anxiously at home to hear how they had got on.

When they arrived at the market, they parked the van in the busiest area they could find. Christmas trees are sold there at Christmas, and in summer there are often vans selling 'Fresh

Newquay Mackerel'. But nobody contested the pitch with them on this cold grey January morning. Having provided themselves with paper bags to put the eggs in, they opened the back of the van, displaying the previously prepared notice 'Fresh Farm Eggs—only 15d. a dozen', and waited for business.

They did not have to wait long. One housewife after another noticed the bonanza, and soon they were both serving as hard as they could go, with a queue stretching right down the side of the van. In an hour, they had cleared the lot, and were stacking up the empty trays before moving off, when the market superintendent came up. He was scandalised. 'What on earth have you been doing?' he cried. 'Selling eggs? In the open market? You can't sell eggs here!' 'I've got news for you,' replied the now triumphant Desmond. 'You can sell them here very well indeed. I've just sold 150 dozen in an hour!' But this, it transpired, was not what the market superintendent meant at all. By setting up the van and offering eggs out of doors, they had contravened goodness knows how many regulations, and richly deserved, he implied, to have their egg trays impounded and their thumbs cut off. At the very least, a spell in the stocks would have been indicated, if Carmarthen in an unwonted fit of progressiveness, hadn't got rid of that amenity some years before. 'Eggs must be sold *inside*,' he explained, 'in the *provision* market. I'll just have to see what I can do about getting you a table.' And as a place luckily became available in the provision market just then, he did, and next Saturday conducted us to a large stall in the provision market, which we have since come to know so well.

We were very ignorant about market techniques. We just stacked the eggs up on the table, displayed our notice, and waited, flapping our arms like cabmen and shivering in the icy draught that came through the open door just by our table. 'Perhaps we should have more notices,' mused Desmond. I jumped at the chance of a little action, hoping to restore my circulation. 'That means more cardboard,' I said hopefully. 'Shall I just nip up to Lodwick's and get a few sheets?' 'No need for that,' replied a strange voice, and turning, we saw that the man from the next stall had approached us. Smiling, he held out some pieces of white cardboard just the size we needed, and when we thanked him, he proceeded to show us the best way of arranging and labelling our goods to catch the customers' eyes. Even better, he very kindly brought over his little Calor gas stove and put it between the two stalls so that we could have a share in its radiant warmth. 'Call me Mac,' he said.

Mac was our mentor in those early market days, and I have sometimes wondered if it was because of his befriending us that we slipped so smoothly into the market routine. We had heard stories about market people—how tough they were, and how aggressive; how they might tip your table up and send your goods crashing to the floor before swaggering off making coarse noises of derision to let down the tyres of your van. I can only say that in the three years we have been in Carmarthen provision market, nobody has done anything like that to us, or to anyone else. Perhaps markets are more violent in big towns.

Desmond did once get involved in a price-cutting war. A man acquired a table in the market from which he began to sell second-quality eggs—cracks, and so on—considerably cheaper than our perfect ones. With some dismay we watched some of our regular customers sidling up to his table, and saw our stacks of eggs too undiminished. Desperate measures seemed indicated, so eventually, catching his eye Desmond took down all our price tickets and slashed them by 5d. Nothing daunted, our rival followed us down, and for the rest of the day it was ding-dong all the way, to nobody's advantage but the customer's. For a week or two the situation looked critical, but eventually it came right. The cracked eggs proved messy and hard to get home even in cartons, and most of our customers returned to us and the better-quality product. Then the man began to leave his stall in the tender care of a bunch of schoolgirls, who were more interested in giggling and throwing cracked eggs at their boyfriends than in attending to business. And so after a few more weeks his enterprise folded, and we returned to the *status quo*.

Over the years we have come to know our regular customers, so that now a day in the market has something of the quality of an 'At Home'. The fragmentary conversation that accompanies the purchase of a couple of dozen eggs twice a week can lead to quite a friendly relationship, but you rarely get to know the customer's name. It was a delightful surprise, therefore, when Rachel started at the Carmarthen Girls' Grammar School, and we went to a meeting of the teachers with the first-form parents, to find that at least twenty of the parents were egg customers, and that for the occasion, they were all wearing identification badges pinned to their fronts. Two-ninths of all parents eating our eggs seemed quite a good proportion, and we toyed with the idea of incorporating it into an advertising slogan, but somehow or other the idea never quite got off the drawing board.

Most of our customers seem to accept us for what we are, which I hope is honest and genuine, but some of the older ones, retired farmers' wives, seem to regard us with the deepest suspicion. 'Are these eggs really fresh with you?' they inquire. 'Are you absolutely sure now?' I suppose they wish to imply that they have forgotten more about eggs and poultry than I shall ever know, and I dare say they are right; but if their experience of the trade from the selling side includes such chicanery as they always seem to be accusing us of, it does them no credit. They may, on the other hand, simply be conscientiously trying to be good and careful shoppers, like those old-fashioned housewives you sometimes hear in butchers' or fishmongers' shops. 'Is the fish nice today, Mr. Blank?' How I long to hear him say 'NO, Madam, on the contrary, it is so far advanced in decay that I deem it a potential danger to public health.' But saner counsels prevail, and stifling a sigh, he answers, 'Yes, Madam; I can particularly recommend the turbot' (presumably because it has the best profit margin); and likewise I, ignoring the implied slight on my integrity, assure the customer that there is not an egg on the stall more than three days old, which is true.

Desmond always does the Wednesday market, where a lot of wholesale transactions go on. Wholesale customers are naturally always looking for the best possible price, and I am not very good at the cut and thrust of selling large lots. I quite often do the gentler Saturday market, and it was on a Saturday one spring that I had my most puzzling brush with a customer.

I had just finished one sale, and had perhaps chatted a few seconds too long over the change. I glanced round, and saw that on the other side of the table there was standing a little woman in a drab green macintosh and a very obvious state of irritation. 'Did I keep you waiting?' I said, apologetically. 'I'm so sorry. What can I get you now?' She glowered at me, unappeased. 'I'm going to tell your husband about you,' she averred. I felt that this was a bit extreme for a wait of perhaps fifteen seconds, but in the cause of peace and goodwill, I apologised again. 'Oh, it isn't only *that*,' she snapped. '*That's* only the last straw. No, it's something you said to my sister earlier on this morning, and I'm going to tell your husband when he comes here next

Wednesday, and you needn't think you're going to get away with
it.'

This flank attack really amazed me. I cast a quick guilty
retrospective glance over the conversations I had had that morning. There couldn't have been many—it was not yet ten o'clock.
'Good morning' I must have said perhaps a dozen times, and
maybe 'It looks a bit better today, doesn't it!'—but surely
nothing actionable, no filth, gossip or blasphemy. 'What did I
say to her?' I demanded. 'You said something *very funny indeed*,
and we're never going to buy eggs with you again. There are
seven of us in our family, and we each buy two dozen large eggs
a week with you, and we're not going to any more. So that's
fourteen dozen eggs a week you've lost because of what you said,
and I'm going to tell your husband too!' And with this parting
shot, she stumped off down the market, leaving me thoroughly
routed, horse and foot. I am really a most peaceable person (ask
any goose), and for a moment I felt quite upset at the venom of
these absurd charges. Then I became aware that the two or three
other customers who had witnessed the incident were all falling
around in various attitudes of suppressed mirth. So I cheered up
and decided to treat it all as a joke. After all, I had said something
'very funny indeed'.

I have never seen the little woman again; she never did come
to tell Desmond what I said to her sister; but still, if the egg sales
are down, I say to Desmond 'That must be the fourteen dozen
large that I lost by careless talk!'

We make various efforts to make our stall look attractive.
Greengrocers' grass spread over the front of the table makes a
background for the stacks of rich brown eggs, and sometimes in
spring I go to the lengths of bringing in a little bunch of flowers,
to help in making what I hope is a fresh, country-ish effect. Simple
jokes go down well, too; once, when a grumbling old man had
insisted that our eggs must be imported French ones, as the price
was so reasonable, Desmond made a notice that said 'My hens
don't speak French' which the customers liked and referred to for
a long time—until Charlie from the stall next door wrote 'Why
not?' on it. On another occasion, when one of our pullets had
laid a really prodigious egg, which must have weighed the best
part of a quarter of a pound, I sent it into the market with
Desmond and told him to write a caption 'If a hen and a half
laid an egg and a half in a day and a half—would it look like

this?' But in the end he didn't. 'I forgot what I was supposed to say' he admitted, 'So I just set it up in the middle of the stall by itself, sitting in a very small egg-cup, and it did its bit in promoting goodwill without saying anything.'

I really enjoy my days at the market. Arriving, if possible, before half past eight, you park your van as near as possible to the market entrance and begin to carry in your eggs. The sun shines through the lofty glass roof, lighting up the bright stalls of flowers, and the piles of fruit. Brown eggs, crates of green cabbage with raindrops still in their folds, tight little bunches of anemones—all the produce looks fresh and lovely, and a sweet, damp smell fills the air as hurrying feet crush dropped leaves and scattered blossoms. Cheerful shouts of greeting and friendly abuse come from your fellow stall-holders up and down the market as everybody bustles about getting unloaded and set up for the day.

By nine o'clock the customers have begun to come, and from then on you are busy, serving hard, until lunch time. Behind our table there is a little blue sweet-and-cigarette kiosk which is run by the two kindest people in the whole market. Phil and Connie Williams have an electric point in their kiosk, and in the generosity of their hearts, they share the benefits of this with all the stall-holders in this part of the market. Cups of soup, cups of tea, buns, sandwiches and cakes appear as if by magic in regular procession at your elbow throughout the day, and if you have to leave your stall for a few minutes during the day, you never lose a sale—Phil or Con will nip out from the kiosk and serve the customer for you.

Charlie, on our right, sells various bargains on his stall, ranging from radios to dish-cloths, duvets to washing-up-liquid, toothpaste to electric car-racing sets. As his goods are often offered at cut prices, people always seem to think that he is open to offers, and some of the offers are very cheeky indeed. But Charlie, who was for many years a Metropolitan mounted policeman, is not easy to bamboozle. I remember one hardened old woman, rather gipsy-looking, who had picked up a bottle of carpet-cleaner, clearly marked 32p. 'Give you 20 pence for this,' she croaked, stuffing it into her pocket and slapping two tens down onto the table. Smoothly, Charlie interposed himself between her and the avenue of retreat she was hoping to sidle down. Towering, he smiled down at her. 'Now listen, my darling,' he said pleasantly, 'I come from London, from a place called Deptford, and I've met people like you before.' Words and tone were amiable, but the woman got the message. She glanced up at him with beady eyes. 'What d'you want, then! What d'you want?' she cried shrilly, defensive. 'I want 32p from you my darling, right here on this table, and then we'll say no more about it.' And Charlie eyed her contemptuously as she paid up, and shuffled off, deflated but still grumbling. 'No difficulty with that lot,' he said. 'I've seen it all before.'

There are several stalls that sell bread and cakes in the market, and one right in front of us wages an incessant war against the pigeons that fly in and out and perch in the high metal struts that support the roof. Crouching protectively over her wares, the bakery woman peers up at the bird perched twenty feet above her head. 'Shoo! Shoo!' she cries, impotently. The pigeon rolls a cold marigold eye at her and flirts its tail dangerously before relenting and flying off to join its mates in the sunshine outdoors. 'It isn't allowed, you know,' she tells me, crossly, relaxing out of her cramped defensive position. But as neither she nor I seem able to make this clear to the pigeons, the harassment continues.

Further up the market is Ralph, who has a nursery garden, and who sells both vegetables and plants on his stall. We carry on long disjointed conversations about such matters as what instrument Vivaldi's double trumpet concerto was originally written for, and which varieties of heather colour up best in winter, and what is the secret of perfect contentment. Each subject necessarily lasts a long time, because one or other of you always has to keep glancing over a shoulder to see if any customers have come to the stall, and sooner or later a customer does come, and when you have boxed up the eggs or weighed out the potatoes and taken the money, you have forgotten the finer points of your argument.

There are various stalls in the market selling antiques, and we always enjoy several chats per market with Pam and Franz up at the top of the market, under the clock. I once nearly did a terrible thing to them. Pam, coming to buy some butter from me early in the day, tendered me a five-pound note which I was unable to change. 'Keep it' she suggested, 'and bring me the change when you've got it.' So I made a mental note that I owed them change, and went on with the day's work. Later, in a lucid interval, I slipped up, but by this time I had forgotten that it had been a fiver, and what I put into Pam's hand, saying 'Here's your change', only made it up to a pound. Pam wears half-spectacles with tortoiseshell rims, and now she regarded me over the top of them very severely indeed. 'Elizabeth!' she said, with forty exclamation marks in her voice. I felt as guilty as if I'd done it on purpose.

Franz is German, and although his English is perfectly collo-quial and fluent, a remaining trace of a German accent gives an additional piquancy to his funny stories and droll sayings. At one general election recently, we were trying to persuade him to vote Liberal, but he seemed hard to convince. 'Last time I vo-oted liberal,' he observed sceptically, 'what I got was Hitler!'

Towards afternoon, the market gets quiet, and there is more time for social visiting to and fro with other stallholders. Some-times the afternoons are very quiet indeed, and the other Charlie, the one from further down the market, who sells materials and speaks seven languages, gets restless. Finally he strides into the centre of the market and makes a general observation in an enormous voice. 'There's more going on in a cemetery on a wet Sunday afternoon than there is in Carmarthen provision market today,' he booms, startling the pigeons, and re-awakening anxiety in the breast of the bakery woman. Everyone agrees with him, and little parties keep leaving for a quiet fifteen minutes in the cool taproom of the Mansel Arms, the market local, which by a lucky dispensation remains open all day on Wednesdays and Saturdays.

Of course we often while away the long afternoons by playing tricks on one another. One day, my customers seemed to be taking an unusual interest in a stack of butter on the front of my stall, but it was hidden from my view by a stack of eggs, and I didn't think anything about it, until one of them said, puzzled but innocent, 'What do you mean by featherless hens, Mrs. Cragoe?' Then I went to look, and found a neatly-written notice propped in front of the butter which said 'All these eggs are laid by featherless hens on our farm in Meidrim'. That was Charlie, of course. Another time he secretly laid out on my stall a most disgusting piece of old brawn, studded with hundreds and thousands, and tastefully decorated with little tufts of fluff picked up from the floor. This time the notice said 'Farmhouse brawn, made only from chicken's heads, on our farm in Meidrim.'

I haven't actually had my revenge, but one day I shall put up a notice on his stall saying 'Everything on this stall discounted 25% on marked prices'. Ralph and I once found a noble offering in the big market rubbish-skip that stands outside the side door, which we put as a mascot on the bonnet of Charlie's car. It was an ox head, discarded by one of the butchers. All the meat had been cut off it, but it still had its muzzle and a little triangle of white curly fur on its brow. Its eyes stared lugubriously, and it looked grand on his car, but unluckily he noticed it and removed it before it had time to make much of an impression.

Another joker—we never discovered who it was—went all round the stallholders' parked vehicles one day putting 'For Sale' notices on them at ridiculously low prices. Lots of people rushed into the market hoping to snap up a bargain two-year-old van for a fiver, but the incident was not in the end very productive of good will.

So, with chatting and jokes and waiting for customers, the afternoon drags its slow length along. Finally someone gives up. Tarpaulins are produced, scales, bacon-slicers, and other valuables are cleaned and locked away in strong boxes. Stallholders produce brushes and sweep the debris from the area immediately surrounding their own stalls. There is none of the early-morning badinage during the clearing up; everyone has his thoughts set on home, and with perfunctory goodnights, we all disperse. And it isn't until you sit down at your own table at home with a cup of tea in front of you that you realise how very tired you really are.

NINE

ACCIDENTS

It is not perhaps generally realised that, actuarially speaking, farming is twice as dangerous as mining. If you spend all your life farming, you are likely to have at least one major accident, as well as a host of minor ones.

When we first started farming, we were constantly surprised by the sight of other farmers' hands. Hardened and worn by toil you expect them to be; brown, calloused, and very strong. But the constant impression we received, as we walked, say, behind a stream of farmers on the way to a farm sale, was that their hands were thick and spongy.

A very short apprenticeship to our job showed us why this should be. In farming, you are using your hands all day, and you hardly ever seize hold of anything that isn't rusty, wet, dirty, resistant and/or stuck, and weighing an absolute minimum of fifty-six pounds. Constant knocks and abrasions make your hands sore until the skin grows thick enough to absorb them, and a daily dip in the hot hypochlorite solution that sterilises milking machines soon swells your epidermis to the classic proportions.

Dealing with animals lays you open to various damages. Leaving aside the problem of kicking cows, there are many possibilities of accident through the sheer size and weight of the creatures. I was nearly knocked out once by a big Friesian we had called Magpie. I was unchaining her after milking one summer evening, and seeing the other cows streaming out of the shed, she was anxious to follow them. As I slipped the chain from her neck, she swung eagerly round and caught me a clout with her great flat face across the side of my head. I saw stars for a few minutes, but at least she didn't have horns.

We took the horns off any cattle we bought that had them, as a precaution against just this kind of accident. It is a job for the vet, and a job for the cool weather, too. Hot weather means flies, which lay their eggs in open wounds, and sickening swarms of maggots result. So autumn, winter or early spring are the dehorning seasons, and on the appointed day, you assemble in the cowshed. First the cow is tied up, with a halter as well as a neckchain, snubbed up short to the bars in front of her stall. Injections of local anaesthetic are then administered, and left to take effect. Then the vets (multiples, often, for this job) nerve themselves for a big effort. One person—the farmer, probably— seizes the patient by the nose, and bends her head round so that the horn is facing frontwards. A vast pair of shears is applied to the base of the horn, and the two vets, standing in the hay passage, apply all their strength to the potent leverage of the long handles. Crunch! Snap! the horn dangles, held only by a little flap of skin, and a fountain of blood from the severed horn arteries jets five feet into the air. Some vets fumble for the cut ends and tie them with gut; others manage to turn them with tweezers so that they twiddle back on themselves. The other horn is dealt with—sulphanilamide powder is dusted over the wound—and away shambles the cow, released, with two nasty-looking holes in the side of her head, and presumably an un-accustomed feeling of lightness.

The holes fill up in due course, and the wounds heal over, though you have to keep a look-out for secondary infections. One of our first lot of Ayrshires must have been recently dehorned, although the white, curly hair of her brow hid the scars, and at first it didn't occur to me to look. 'There's something curious about Tommy,' I used to say to Desmond. 'She looks well and she's milking well, but her breath smells like Danish Blue cheese. I notice it every time I go to tie her up. Whatever can it be?' What it was, of course, was not her breath, but a little pocket of infection in a horn-stub, and it cleared up with a very few applications of sulphanilamide powder once we had realised where the trouble lay.

Although cows sometimes bellow, indicating pain, while the horn is actually being cut off, they don't seem to suffer any after-effects. Hawthorn, indeed, went on butting the sides of the other cows without a day of intermission when she had her spikes off, leaving them smudged with her blood in the process. It looked agony, but it didn't even make her flinch. All we seemed to be able to detect in her mien was indignation at the fact that it no longer seemed to work so well as hitherto.

As well as making them safer for human beings to handle,

97

dehorning makes cows less able to damage one another. I shall never forget a cow called Jet on the farm where I was a pupil, and the squirt of bright blood that came from her teat into the strip cup one night, when a mate of hers had given her a good hike in the udder.

Dehorning is much less traumatic if it is done to calves when they are young, when it should really be called disbudding. An instrument rather like an electrically-heated soldering iron is used for this, in effect, a heated metal tube with a sharp edge. After an injection of local anaesthetic, the calf is firmly held, and the growth that will become the horn is burnt out. When the little white particle, smaller than a marble, falls onto the floor at your feet, you know that that puts paid to all possibility of growth for that horn at least. Calves look rather pathetic for a few hours after the operation, because the injection that protects them from pain also immobilises the nerve that controls their ears, and until it passes off, they look very droopy. But I have never known a calf to show any signs of suffering afterwards, or to go off its feed, or lose condition. Farmers are full of terrible stories of people who have had their cheeks ripped open by a cow accidentally catching a horn-tip in their mouth when they are bending to tie her up; we felt that there were enough risks we couldn't avoid, without exposing ourselves to those we could do something about.

Breaking in heifers to the milking machine, to which they usually object, puts you in the way of a few kicks here and there, though some take to it more easily than others. Byron, a farmer friend in Meidrim, had a particularly awkward heifer once, and having heard that he was having a rough passage with her, I asked him, at a chance rencontre, how she was settling down. 'I've milked her more or less lying on her back twice a day for the last fortnight, but I think she's beginning to come a bit sooky at last!'

Late in our dairying career, we discovered the Dalton kick-bar, a cunningly-designed bit of angled metal that fits very easily over the cow's back, tucks under her flank, and immobilises her stifle joint. With one of these on each side, she can wriggle, but if they are properly adjusted, she really can't lash out, and the horrid possibility of a broken leg for the person milking her is much diminished.

Before we came across this, however, we had experimented

with most of the traditional methods of keeping a recalcitrant animal still. You can tie a rope very tightly around her body; to make that more effective, you can use it to tie a plank of wood flat along the length of her spine. You can tie one of her front legs up, so that to kick you she would have to balance on two; but all these methods have their disadvantages, and battling with a heifer is a great waste of time. We always tried to prepare our heifers, which were hand-tame anyway, for milking by getting them used to having their bags stroked and rubbed, but presumably a freshly-calved bag is more sore or more ticklish than a slack one; at any rate, however you prepare them, there are some heifers who just don't like the machine, and take great pains to remove it.

I was milking by myself one night and I had come to the turn of the most freshly-calved heifer. Her name was Topbush Atalanta, and she was a big, black animal, of noble proportions. 'That's a very rich-looking heifer,' one of our neighbours had said, expressively, when he saw her in the field shortly before she calved. But rich-looking or not, she didn't like the machine, and tied up with every rope I could lay hands on, she was strenuously trying to remove it. It was a very hot evening and I knew I must be scarlet as I battled with her in the stall. To and fro she swung, wriggling, stamping and fidgeting, while I, dripping with sweat, was flung to and fro with her, one hand on her tail and the other on the machine insecurely attached to her udder. In the middle of my preoccupation, I became aware that somebody was standing in the door of the cowshed. 'Ah! Good!' I thought. 'Someone who will say "Let me hold her tail up and keep her still, so that you can concentrate on keeping the machine on her".' But not so. After watching me critically for a moment or two as I flew hither and thither like the proverbial flea on a cow's tail, my visitor spoke. She had a flat, Black-Country voice. 'Excuse me,' she said, 'have you got time to get me half a dozen eggs?'

Most of our neighbours have survived hair-raising accidents; Wynford Cefn turned the tractor over onto himself when mowing a field on his father's farm, and lay there for over an hour with the power-operated mower going full blast only inches from his face before help came. Then it was only by grace of the fact that a woman in a house within earshot of the field he was working in noticed that the noise of the tractor seemed to be coming only from one place, instead of moving steadily up and down the field as it had been doing before. He had a broken pelvis, a broken leg, but after a spell in hospital, he emerged as good as new, and as far as one can see is in no way hampered in his farming by these old injuries.

After the accident has happened, you can always point a finger at your mistake. We all try to develop good safety habits, but, working against time as you always seem to be, there is a fatal tendency to take short cuts, and sooner or later you get caught out.

Everybody knows, for instance, that you should disconnect the power-take-off of the tractor before making an adjustment to a powered implement, but how many people, habitually using such things, can lay a hand on their heart and honestly swear that they do? The forces engendered by a tractor engine, of, say, 65 hp, are so great that the human body crumples like touchwood against them; but every year experienced farmers fall foul of them and pay the penalty to a greater or lesser extent.

If you were to have asked Elwyn, for instance, twelve years ago, whether or not it was safe to clear a choked baler without disconnecting the power supply, I am sure he would have said it was dangerous—foolhardy, indeed; yet, baling for a neighbour, with rain in the offing and the pressure on in good earnest, that is exactly what he did. Suddenly free, the machine thumped down before he could get out of the way, catching his arm and pulling him violently forward so that he hit his head against its outer casing. The shock is so great in cases of substantial injury that you do not at first feel pain in the damaged area, and dazed by the blow on the head, Elwyn did not notice that his arm was broken. His attention was drawn to it by the unexpected sight of his watch, with its metal strap severed, lying on the ground under the baler. In some surprise he glanced at his left wrist, and saw to his horror that the lower part of his arm was hanging off at a right angle. 'The chap I was baling for rushed off to get help,' he told me. 'But I was beginning to feel a bit faint, and I thought I'd better get a bit nearer to civilisation while I still could. I was a bit concussed from the bump on the head I'd given myself, and I couldn't see much, but I found that if I tipped my head right back and sort of squinted sideways, I could just see enough to get along. So I set off—it was three fields from the house—but before I got far, I could feel a kind of bump! bump!

against my left hip. I looked down, and it was the broken bit of my arm, dangling there, banging against me at every step. So I picked it up with the other hand as best I could, and set off again. I remember thinking at the time what a damn fool I must look, shuffling along like that with my head all on one side.'

Ten years and several operations later, Elwyn has a fairly serviceable left arm again, and not only he, but everyone who knows him, is careful when fiddling with powered implements. We all learn from one another's accidents; the thing I did has caused many a ripple of horror through people who say to themselves, 'I've done that many a time! It could easily have happened to me!'

We were making silage at the time, and the accident happened while we were attaching the tractor to a trailer full of grass, preparatory to tipping it. The draw-bar of the tractor has a double end with a hole right through it, and that of the trailer, a single one; you back up the tractor till the holes are perfectly aligned, and then, slotting a hitch-pin down through them all, you are left with a kind of draw-bar sandwich, tractor-implement-tractor, firmly held in place by the pin. It was my job to put the pin in, and the alignment looked perfect, but for some reason I could not force the pin down the hole. Thinking that Desmond on the tractor was looking round watching what I was up to, I put an exploratory forefinger in to see what the obstruction could possibly be. But there are some holes a finger should never be introduced to. Thinking to himself, 'She can't get the pin in— I'll have to re-align it,' Desmond let the clutch in and moved the tractor forward.

'My finger! My finger! You've caught my finger!' I shrieked, feeling the enormous pressure, and realising that it must be broken. But I must say I was truly amazed when he reversed again and I pulled out—nothing. The finger lay on the yard beneath the draw-bar, looking dirty and rather pathetic, as it was already wearing a grubby piece of elastoplast on some other, more trifling wound.

As accidents go, I was lucky in that mine was relatively pain-less. We went down to the hospital, where a doctor tidied me up on the left-hand side, and a nice, nice casualty sister talked to me on the right. It was the left forefinger, which is lucky, too, as I am right-handed. But it leaves me with an ugly hand, and I often notice small children looking at it with horrified fascination.

But it was Desmond, who likes to do things in style, who had potentially the most dreadful accident—again, due entirely to his own fault, a knowledge that is very unconsoling.

He had gone down, one Sunday morning, to spread a load of hen muck in Parc y Mynydd, our one field on the other side of the main road. We were paddock grazing at that time, which meant that all the fields were divided into one-acre blocks by a system of electric fences. To get to the paddock where he intended to spread the muck, Desmond had to get through several others, and after stopping the tractor about four times to get off and open a way through the wire, he got careless. The top part of Parc y Mynydd slopes fairly steeply, but it flattens out as it gets nearer Meidrim, and it was on this flatter bit that Desmond drew up to open the last fence. To save trouble—oh, had he but known what trouble he was going to cause himself!—he did not put on the handbrake, but went to open the wire leaving the tractor standing free, with the engine running. Now a full load of muck, weighing perhaps two tons, exerts quite a pressure behind a tractor, and as he bundled the wire out of the way he saw that the tractor had begun to move, and was now making its way, slowly, but accelerating, towards the bottom of the field. Muttering a curse, he ran after it, caught hold of the steering wheels, and put one foot on the step to climb aboard. But the other foot slipped, and was caught by the big back wheel, and before he knew what was happening, he was drawn inexorably onto the ground, and rolled out like a piece of pastry. It went on to him over his toe, ran right up his body and off over his face. With the last remnant of his strength he rolled away from the following wheels of the muckspreader, and lay there, thinking he was going to die.

But death did not come. And after a few seconds, he tried to take a breath, and found he could. It hurt him terribly to expand his crushed rib-cage, but successive breaths came easier, and, not wishing to lie there indefinitely, he thought he had better try to crawl up the field towards home. His legs worked, he found, though feebly; and when, after a hundred yards or so, he ventured to clamber to his feet, he found that his back was in one piece too.

The children, playing in the yard, looked up in horror as this

102

filthy, torn, bloody apparition shambled into view, and when he told them what had happened they rushed in to me, where I was washing-up in the kitchen, screaming, 'The tractor went right over Daddy! The tractor went right over Daddy!'

The hospital in Carmarthen is a big, modern one, with excellent facilities, but what endears it to us is the amazingly homely atmosphere, village-like, that embraces you when need drives you through its portals. The ambulance men lifted the battered Desmond as if he was their brother; the porter who wheeled his trolley to the X-ray room was a man we knew quite well, who used to deliver cattle-cake to our farm, in a previous job; even the trolley itself, we noticed, was one made by a firm whose managing director was the father of one of our friends. It was the very antithesis of impersonal.

Desmond's X-rays showed, amazingly, that only one bone was broken—his right cheek, which had a depressed fracture—where the tyre had finally slipped off him. Damage to soft organs is not so easy to spot, and we had some anxious hours while his bodily functions gradually re-asserted themselves. But he had been astonishingly lucky, and apart from the general crushing, which gave him considerable pain for a long time, no damage had been done. The tractor weighs two tons six hundredweights, and to this must be added the substantial weight of the load of muck, transferred through the draw-bar. The ground was fairly soft from recent rain, and this must have saved him, but at that, it must be the sort of escape you can fairly call miraculous!

It is at a time of crisis like this that you see all that is best in the Welsh social tradition. I am sure that that evening and the following morning I must have received forty visits and telephone calls offering help. And the offers were real, and concrete, too—not vague generalisations. 'Would you like the boys to come down and do the milking for you until your husband is better?' 'How are you fixed for a lift to the hospital this evening?' 'Would you like me to stay with the children while you go to visit him?' 'I know you can't drive—I was wondering if you'd like me to drive the van in on market days for you till Desmond gets back?' and so on.

Lots of people did me kindnesses then for which I shall always be grateful, and very luckily for me, my cousin Bruce came to stay for a week, which solved the driving problem. Desmond had to go to Morriston hospital, near Swansea, for an operation to reduce the fracture of his cheek, but he was home inside a week, and tentatively working again inside another. That is very characteristic of a farmer. A worker in an industrial organisation who has an accident tends to make the most of it. There may be compensation in it for him; at the very least, he will be 'on the sick' for a while, having a paid holiday until he is perfectly recovered. But farmers are independent. Although they know their neighbours will help them in times of trouble, they hate to be a nuisance, and the tradition of stoicism which still lingers in farming inclines them to play down their injuries and pains, rather than to flaunt them, in the hope of attracting sympathy.

But before I leave the subject of Desmond's accident, I must record one man's reaction to it, which came back to me by devious ways and has caused me many a smirk: 'Yes,' he is reported to have said, when he heard that Desmond was in hospital, 'when I was driving past this morning I saw Cragoe coming out of his field, very white, and covered in blood. But I didn't like to stop.' *Quelle délicatesse!*

Inevitably, farming develops the 'manly' qualities in men, because in farming the buck stops with the individual. One of the concomitants of being your own boss is that you have to take the responsibility for yourself too; when things go wrong, you must put them right yourself. There is nobody else to do so.

And problems, by and large, are soluble. This was one of the lessons our experienced neighbours taught us in situations that seemed so hopeless that we were near giving up in despair. It was water that was our chief trouble in Penllwynplan. The hens are catered for by an electric pump worked by a float-switch that pumps up water from a spring in the dip. It is a temperamental beast, but it generally works, if you keep your fingers crossed. But the cattle in the cowshed got the water in their drinking-bowls from a well, and that was a constant source of trouble. Gravity-feeding into a header tank in the buildings, the water came down the field in an old copper pipe, and as the passage of time had made this porous, the well constantly lost its siphonage. For a year or two we limped along, by using the milking-machine pump to restore the siphonage first thing every morning, but the porosity increased, and one morning, suck and drag as we might, we couldn't get any water.

'Replace the copper with alkathene, and all will be well,' we thought, so Desmond drove off to St. Clears in the redoubtable mini van, and came back with five hundred yards of the stuff, and the fixings. To meet the emergency we laid it on top of the ground and planned to bury it later. Desmond is quite a handy plumber at a pinch, and he fixed the end near the buildings into the system, and the various joints up the field, without any trouble. Then he went up to examine the end that had to dip down into the well. One thinks of the top of a well—at least I used to—as a neat round hole, perhaps with a little coping round it, or even a little roof and a bucket on a winding thing. But our well was not like that. A small square had been fenced off, at the top of Cae Uchaf, and there, surrounded by rampant brambles, was the opening to the well. It was covered by very rotten sleepers, and was clearly a big and irregular hole.

By this time Elwyn had noticed that we were engaged in some kind of unusual activity and he and Claude, Dai's brother, who worked for him, came across to see if they could help. 'Those sleepers are very rotten,' said Elwyn. 'Go get the tractor and some ropes, Claude; we'll pull them off from a distance, then we can check if the lip is safe before anybody goes on it to look down the well.' Exposed, the well looked horrid—a great yawning hole, in shale rather than rock, which veered off sideways instead of going straight down.

Elwyn's cousin Glyn with his brother Eric joined us at this stage, and a conference was held to discuss the best course of action. It was agreed that the well must be sounded, to see how much water was in it, and as the overhang made this impossible from ground level, it was evident that somebody must go down. More ropes were fetched, and ladders, and when they had been carefully lowered down, lashed at the top to a tractor for safety, Claude made the first descent into the clammy depths.

It was mid-afternoon by this time, and the thirsty cows, waterless in their shed, were lowing dreadfully. But we were braced by the thought of their immediate relief as Claude reappeared to say that he had located the in-pipe, coming through about eight feet down, and that if the alkathene could be put down over the well lip, it could be connected to the bit of copper, still sound, that dropped down into the water itself, some forty feet down. Hacksaws and stilson wrenches were produced, and when everybody had been down the well to make their own assessment of the situation, the joint was duly made.

At five o'clock, we started the pump motor, and watched the

pressure gauge rise, as we waited confidently for the splosh of water falling into the header tank.

Nothing happened.

'It may be a bit slow,' said Elwyn, encouragingly. 'It's got a long way to pull it.' So we waited and waited; but still nothing happened. Finally, Desmond switched off the motor, and we looked at one another in silence. I didn't know what we ought to do next—to release those poor thirsty beasts, and drive them in the dark, down to drink at the Meidrim river, or what? What I really wanted to do was to sit down and howl like a dog. But suddenly, Elwyn spoke. 'I've been thinking,' he said. 'That's a very deep well. And there must be some reason for that pipe going into it eight feet down, instead of at the top, which is what you'd expect. And it just came into my mind that somebody once told me that a siphon won't work over 40 feet. So maybe that's what the trouble is here. And I think the best thing we can do is to get up that field again and find out.'

So up the field they toiled again, in the black dark and the bitter east wind, and by the light of the tractor headlamps, dug a trench at the point where they hoped to pick up the pipe where it began to dive through the hillside. And as virtue and hard work must eventually be rewarded, at last they found it, and, sawing it off, drew it out, poked the alkathene through the hole thus made, and re-fastened all the joints.

I was in the house when they finally started the motor to try once more to remake the siphon. A black gloom of depression was on me—were we, after all, to have to go to bed and leave those poor thirsty cows till the morning? It seemed unthinkable. But then the door flew open, and Dai bounded in. He was radiant. 'Come out here quick, Missis,' he cried, 'and listen to this.' So I hurried out, to hear what sounded then the most musical sound in the world—the sustained splash of a strong stream of water falling into the tank, and the steady noise of twenty thirsty cows drinking, drinking, drinking.

TEN

THE WELSH ARE...

English friends who visit us often ask us if we are very conscious of the nationhood of the Welsh. 'Are they so different from the English?' they ask. And after twelve years of living in Wales, we feel more and more inclined to answer: 'Yes, they are.'

Wales, to me, is an intensely romantic country. My spine prickles when I cross the border, homeward bound, after a foray into England. I love reading old Welsh legends, about heroes like Cilhwch, who rode 'a grey horse, four winters old, shell-hooved, and with bridle bit of gold', and who carried a battle-axe that would draw blood from the wind, and was 'swifter than the swiftest dewdrop from the stalk to the ground, when the dew is heaviest in June'. There is something essentially Celtic in this hyperbolic imagery. I hear it when Dai comments on somebody's well-conditioned cattle. 'Shining like a bottle they are with him,' he says. Or Elwyn, speaking of a man who once tried to cheat him over a pig deal, will say 'I'd know that face if I saw it in a crow's beak.' I don't suppose either of them reads the *Mabinogion*, the most famous collection of Welsh fairy stories, but the poetry has not gone entirely underground in them. 'Whiter than Eyryri's snows were they' says the chronicler, describing Pryderi's deerhounds, 'save that their ears were as red as foxgloves,' and a man of our times, describing a sheepdog to me, once said that she was 'As blue as a pigeon, with a silver eye.' It is hard to imagine a Saxon being so lyrical.

People in Wales are friendlier, too, I think, than people in England. Looking back on my year as a pupil in Shropshire, I can remember every cow by its face and name, but not a single one of the neighbours. Here, your lives intertwine; you are beholden to somebody for something almost every day of the week.

I was talking to Howell one day, years ago, standing by his churn-stand, quite early in the morning. He was answering everything I said, but clearly with only half his attention; his mind was distracted, and he kept looking up the track towards his neighbour's farm, which lay out of sight behind a spur of woodland. Finally he came to a decision. 'I think if you'll excuse me I'd better go and see what's happened to Dewi,' he said. 'I don't want to be interfering, but he's never as late as this putting his milk on the stand. He does live by himself, and you never know, he may have had an accident.'

This kind of caring is an exceedingly Welsh characteristic. Nobody could die in this village and lie unnoticed until the milk-bottles piled up on their doorstep. And it must not be thought that this business of everybody being his brother's keeper happens by chance, or is motivated by mere inquisitiveness. In a Welsh country area, it is considered proper behaviour to offer help; to pass by on the other side, with urban indifference, would be unthinkable.

One morning, a few months after our arrival, we were in the yard, struggling to make a refractory muck-spreader do its job. That is to say, Desmond was struggling, and I was making clucking noises of sympathy, and holding myself available, mate-style, to fetch anything that might be needed in the way of spanners and oil-cans. Elwyn, driving past, noticed that we were 'on stop' and came over to see what the trouble was. Between them, he and Desmond put it right, but it took a good two hours, and we felt exceedingly obliged to him. But when we thanked him, he brushed it aside as nothing at all. 'You're in Wales now!' he said, with that half-humorous, half-sardonic lift of the eyebrow that characterises your true Celt.

There are about five hundred people in our parish, and of course, everybody knows virtually everybody else. As well as being all of one set in so far as they are all Meidrim people, they are bound together in other associations. The church and chapels are lively, vigorous organisms which themselves give rise to sub-sets, like the choir, the Mothers' Union, and the Sunday School. Other groupings are formed by the W.I., the Young Farmers' Club, and even things like the darts and quoits teams of the local pubs. People are constantly shuffled into fresh patterns and associations, and nobody need remain lonely.

In summer these organisations make up outings, and two or three coaches full of revellers often sweep past the farm in the early morning, bound for the bright lights of Cardiff and

Aberafon. I always think of Laurie Lee and Dylan Thomas as I see them go. Rain does not seem to damp the travellers' spirits. Surrounded by scenery every day of their lives, what they want to do on an outing is almost independent of the weather. Amusement arcades for the young, a different and bigger assortment of shops for the older, and a good fish-and-chip shop for all adds up to a good outing. Crates of beer in the bus, and one or two stops at pubs on the way home constitute the men's entertainment.

In winter, each organisation begins to collect names for a dinner. Membership of the host body does not seem to be a *sine qua non* for going to the dinner; anybody can come—everybody does. It usually costs about £2 a head, which includes a coach there and back. The dinners are exceedingly convivial; turkey is usually on the menu, and afterwards the room is cleared, and the party continues, with dancing, drinking, games, and—of course—singing.

Singing comes as naturally to the Welsh as breathing, there is no doubt about that. The eisteddfod is a vigorous living tradition, and from the age of three or four, children are encouraged to get up on the platform and compete in it. Primary and secondary schools alike expect their children to support the Eisteddfodau organised by the Urdd, the national youth movement of Wales; everyone can do something, play on an instrument, sing, dance, or recite.

Some children are hacked round the eisteddfod circuit by their proud parents like mini professionals, a practice which tends to develop in them a rather unappetising precocity. One curly-headed moppet of about eight who swept the board at our local Eisteddfod, had a real chapel-style vibrato, and a sickening way of shaking her curls as she sang, with winsome smirk, and head on one side. But the judges obviously liked it. Other children retain a surprising freshness, and when their turn comes, simply stand up and sing, spontaneous as a blackbird. Little silver cups are often presented, and some children have a shelf-full before they have left primary school.

Another entirely Welsh function, often put on by a church or chapel as a fund-raising effort, is a 'Cawl Supper'. Cawl, which means roughly 'broth', is the national dish of Wales. In some ways it is like the French *pot-au-feu*, but the meat involved is usually a piece of home-cured bacon. Lamb is an acceptable substitute, but beef is rarely used. The piece of meat is boiled in a big pan—traditionally a 'crochan' or cauldron, but nowadays more usually just an ordinary large saucepan. The broth is skimmed a few times, and vegetables, including potatoes, are added as it cooks. Then the whole panful is simmered quietly until it is done. Any vegetable in season can go into the pot, but the *sine qua non*, 'without which you can't call it cawl,' they tell me, is some parsley, and some leeks.

It is in the method by which it is eaten that cawl really differs from other national stew dishes. Your authentic traditional Welshman sits down to his meal armed with a wooden spoon and a white pudding basin. This is not a bit of self-conscious revivalist whimsy; it is just the way cawl is eaten, and you can see the table laid in this way any night of the week in several houses in this village. First he consumes a bowlful of the broth, with a bit of bread. The second course is a bowlful of the potatoes and vegetables, with a little more broth as gravy. A piece of mild cheese is often put into the middle of this, where it melts succulently among the hot vegetables. Finally, he eats a few slices of the meat, for which I suppose, he must avail himself of a knife and fork.

The mild Caerphilly cheese is particularly suited to this kind of use, and Welsh people eat a great deal of it. A traditional Welsh breakfast dish, called 'bara te', is prepared by buttering a slice of bread and breaking it up into a basin. A hot, sweet, milky cup of tea is poured over it, and a lump of cheese, again, is set to dissolve in the middle. I have never been able to face this; 'It turns on me,' as they say round here, but dietetically it seems well enough balanced, and perhaps the flavours are no more bizarrely associated than in my own Yorkshire habit of eating cheese with a piece of fruit cake.

We went to a Cawl Supper at a little country church near here, with two friends, who belonged to it. We didn't know what to expect, but we enjoyed it immensely.

Standing in the ticket queue outside the church hall, we were aware of the bustle of preparation within. Light spilled out of the windows, and from the kitchen end, billows of savoury steam contrasted fragrantly with the raw November air. Cars were parked everywhere, nose to tail along the narrow lanes, as over a hundred people gathered, prepared to do justice to the good fare.

Inside, long trestles had been set up, temptingly laid with

110

traditional delicacies. Breads of all kinds seem to be a local speciality, and buttery platefuls of date-and-walnut, malt loaf, and curranty 'bara brith' jostled the maids-of-honour, melting Welshcakes and flyaway sponges that every Welshwoman makes so well.

The cawl had been cooking all day in a great electric boiler in the kitchen. For ease of serving, the meat on this occasion had been cut into small pieces before being cooked, and it and the vegetables had completely 'gone into' the broth, which was thick and rich. By a miracle of timing, the red and perspiring committee of cooks decided that it was *au point* just as the vicar announced that it really was time he said grace; members of the congregation, dressed as chefs, carried it round in great steaming tureens, and then it was up spoons and away. A day of fresh air, culminating in an evening milking for most of the people present, had put an edge on everybody's appetite. Greediness was interpreted charitably as compliment to the cooks, and for those who wanted three bowlsful, there was enough and to spare.

With the first edge off our appetites we began to devote more of our attention to conversation, and a quick burst of 'That's who he is' soon put us on terms of recognition with all the people at our table. One of the beauties of living in a small community is that everybody you meet is aunty or cousin or brother's son's girlfriend to somebody you already know, so you start the acquaintanceship with a certain amount of background in common.

A short pause for conversation and assimilation was followed by a renewal of vigour as we moved to decimate the contents of the ranked plates. Tea was passed round, and finally replete, we drifted away from the tables in chatting groups, while busy helpers rearranged the seating for the next part of the programme.

Three little children, with guitars almost as big as themselves, were produced, and sang very prettily in Welsh. The hall was darkened, and somebody showed slides of an exotic holiday. But the crowning performance of the evening was given by a young man of about twenty, a fresh-faced country boy, who stood up on the platform and gave us a comic recitation in Welsh. I think it was about a dog who jumped into a larder and stole a joint of meat; the audience loved it, and applauded him rapturously, and so good was his timing, so droll his expression, that we found ourselves joining in the laughter even without understanding what was being said.

Country entertainments of this kind are, it is true, unsophisticated, but it is worth remembering that the original meaning of that word was 'spoiled by over-elaboration'. I much prefer going to a concert or play in which I can see my friends and acquaintances from the neighbourhood doing their bit to sitting watching a nationally famous comedian on television cracking his slick but weary jokes. Professional smoothness is not all in entertainment; local colour can more than compensate for its absence.

Reared from infancy in an atmosphere of participation, the Welsh are nearly all good performers when it comes to entertainment, and any assembly can put on a show. A party of miners was in our market local, the Mansel Arms, one Saturday. Parties often come from quite distant parts to avail themselves of our unusual licensing laws in Carmarthen, and this bunch were well away with their singing when we came in for our usual after-market drink. Sometimes it was a chorus, sometimes a solo; one couple sang a duet; and the matter that they were singing varied too. A hymn, a pop song, a folk song, and part of a chorus from the *Messiah* followed one another in quick succession. And whoever was singing, and whatever they were singing, they gave it everything they had got. No false modesty, no trace of self-consciousness inhibited them, and the very tankards hanging behind the bar trembled on their hooks with the force of the vibrato. Anybody who could harmonise, did, often going above the melody to add a descant line. One stout, blue-cheeked man in his fifties sang with so much 'hwyl' that the tears ran down his closed eyes and dripped into his pint. It must have been quite a moving song, for I saw several people producing handkerchiefs and giving their eyes a quick dab at the end.

Whenever I hear Welsh singing, unmistakable as it is, and particularly if I am away from home, I feel a thrill of pride, of identification. 'That's our lot,' I think to myself.

A good sing is a good thing, think the Welsh, but a good religious sing is even better. Many chapels hold a kind of singing festival, called a 'Gymanfa Ganu', and people drive miles to take part in them. They are widely advertised, and plenty of people who don't belong to that particular chapel will make a point of going to the gymanfa, for the pleasure of joining in with a good, hearty, well-conducted choir. Another form of church or chapel entertainment is the 'Pwnc'. This is basically a competitive quiz for young people on Biblical questions, and people get surprisingly steamed up and partisan about it sometimes.

We often have to smile when people tell us how boring it must be living in the country. Nothing could be further from the truth. If you had the energy and the will, you could attend some kind of function within a twenty mile radius every night of your life, winter and summer alike.

Rodeos, for instance, with boys and girls trying to ride steers and unbroken mountain ponies, are often held in summer, but an unfortunate accident in which a pony broke a leg and had to be destroyed has caused people to look again at the ethics of this sport, and it may not be allowed much longer.

Terrier racing, however, can surely have no opponents. Strong, sturdy little dogs of the Jack Russell type, are held in a line by their handlers, while their interest is whetted by a fox's brush. which is flourished temptingly in front of them. When a suitable pitch of excitement has been generated, the tail is drawn up the field on a string. Released, the dogs hurl themselves after it, as it whisks out of sight into a drainpipe. The pipe is only big enough for one dog to get into, so there is no need of a photo finish—the dog in the pipe is the winner.

There are meetings for various different kinds of car and motorcycle racing. There are expeditions, organised by a few friends, for simple pleasures like nutting, blackberrying, or picking cockles. Dai used to enjoy all this kind of thing, and he came into the kitchen one morning rubbing his hands with a satisfied air. 'By damn! It's going to be a good week this week!' he said 'Scrambling Monday; cockling with Gwynfor on Tuesday, because the tide'll be right; and there's a grass-track meeting at Hendre on Saturday. Think of it—scrambling, cockling, and grass-track racing all in one week!' Scrambling, cockling, and grass-track racing—the phrase has passed into our family folklore, where it denotes good things pressed down, shaken together and running over. I suppose it is the same sort of thing W. H. Davies was thinking about when he wrote 'Lord! How rich and great the times are now!'

Meidrim is in the middle of one of the most Welsh areas of Wales. Welsh is nearly everybody's mother tongue, and most of the primary schools are taught through the medium of Welsh, particularly in the first two years. Our children both had to learn

Welsh when they started school at the age of four and a half, and did so in a few weeks without any apparent difficulty. Welsh is based on a very different phonetic system from English, however, and the effect on their spelling of English words was very quaint for a few years. I kept one or two of their more bizarre productions, like this letter that Rachel wrote to my sister when she was six. She already had a doll called Barby, and my sister had sent her, for Christmas, a talking doll called Ken, widely advertised as Barby's boy-friend, and a doll's bed. This is what Rachel wrote:

> Dear Jilian,
> Thangcew very very much for Ken wen he talkt
> to mummy hse lafd her hed of becos she laect
> it so much. at this very momunt his in bed with
> Barby. I thingk h'es in love with her
> Enewa, let hem get on with it.
>   lov from
>   Rachel.

I am particularly fond of enewa.

One of Matthew's better efforts was a list for Santa Claus of suggestions for Christmas presents, in which he wrote that he would like 'A ghatar, a nhaits helmet, and a book about slaves'. (Sinister, that, as my mother remarked when she read it.)

Of course, everybody speaks English as well, and gatherings like farm sales are conducted in English, but the auctioneer often slips into Welsh for the jokes. It is quite frustrating when everyone bursts into a roar of laughter at some quick aside, and you can't understand it. We have picked up a little Welsh, but not enough to appreciate quick-fire witticisms in the local patois.

By the same token, many of the people in the village cannot understand a more classic form of their native tongue. I have often asked, for instance, 'What did the Vicar preach about at the Harvest Festival?' only to be answered, 'I don't know. It's deep Welsh with him—Bible Welsh. I can't understand that.'

Welsh speakers from opposite ends of the country are often obliged to communicate in English because their dialects are mutually unintelligible. Gwill, from Dolgellau, conducts his business in Carmarthen cattle mart in English for this reason. Presumably this diversity has remained because Wales has not, since she was first united as a country, had a single royal court to give a lead as to the 'correct' form of words. London, for us

English, became quite early on the social and administrative apex of the country, and the English of the south-east—Chaucer's kind of English—gradually conquered all the others. But in Wales, for many centuries there were several small kingdoms and principalities, disputing among themselves for the leadership. And then—Westminster. So no one dialect ever gained an absolute predominance.

It often strikes us that the very basis of social intercourse is different in Wales from in England. Perhaps this is because they were never so thoroughly worked over by the Normans. The ruins of the castles are to be seen; the bold bad barons must have existed; but the next link in the feudal chain is conspicuous by its absence. A squirearchy, with its very real power, and its insistence on the 'us and them' principle, is strikingly absent from the area. You do not find a dominant 'big house' in every small village here, as you do in rural England. The much more egalitarian tribal society peeps through here and there. You have to earn respect by your merit, it is no use expecting it to come, as it often does in England, through your bank book.

A prodigious concern with relationships is one of the characteristics of the clan system, and the 'that's who he is' syndrome in modern Wales presumably takes the place of the long genealogical poems of earlier times. I have heard a theory that the striking Welsh preoccupation with funerals confers a social benefit in that it provides an opportunity for people who do not meet in the course of everyday life—people, perhaps, who used to know each other, but who have moved apart—to get together, and get up to date on one another's news.

Like all Celtic peoples, the Welsh seem to be attuned to an oral rather than a literary culture. They are highly articulate. Any old farmer, waylaid by a television interviewer in a market to give his opinion on a matter of agricultural policy, or what have you, seems to be able to turn round and deliver a five-minute flow of rhetoric at the drop of a hat. 'Um', 'er', and 'yer know', phrases so beloved of English interviewees, seem to have been left out of the Welsh language.

A ready tongue means a quick wit, and repartee comes naturally to everybody. One elderly woman was recounting to me a conversation she had been having with an English visitor. "Mrs. Davies," he says to me, "I see you got a lavender bush growing up by the back door. I'm surprised at you. Don't you know that lavender kills passion?" "No!" I says to him. "Does it? Thats what it must be, then!"'

In English too they are deft with words, and I like some of the local dialects usages. 'The car went on stop with us' they will say, rather than 'we had a breakdown'. Children in the local school playground are 'making shapes' at one another rather than making faces, and as the little boys rush round firing imaginary pistols at one another they cry 'Pang! Pang!' rather than bang. Instead of 'I was half finished', a man will say 'it was on half with me'. Inverting the word-order is another habit, and when I asked a woman who had nettled herself badly the previous day how her stings were getting on, she replied 'Itching and smarting both with me they are today.'

Surprisingly, in a country so concerned with religion, swearing is universal, and carries no offence at all. Men, indeed, often swear about things they feels quite gently towards. One of Elwyn's casual workers remarked to him once 'I shan't be in this afternoon. I've got to go to the hospital. My bloody aunty's had a stroke. Very bad with her too, poor fucker.'

Perhaps it was as a defence against the hardness of their lives in times gone by that people developed such a sense of humour. Perhaps it is simply the volatile nature of the Celt. 'There was plenty of sweating in those days,' says John Davies, Lan, Elwyn's father, recounting tales of old times. 'But plenty laughing too.' But though times are easier now, a Welshman is always ready to see the funny side of things.

This was fortunate in my first encounter with Mr. Davies himself. I had occasion to telephone Elwyn, and not knowing that he was *Richard* Elwyn Davies, I had spent a frustrating twenty minutes tracking him down among the sixteen pages of Davieses in the telephone book. When I did finally get through, a man's voice, disguised, I thought, very cautiously said 'Hello.' Elwyn is famous for his telephone jokes, so thinking I was on the receiving end of one, I said, 'Come off it, you miserable old wretch, I've had enough trouble trying to track you down.' There was a dreadful pause, and the voice said, very coldly, 'This is the old man speaking. Elwyn's father.' Horror! What had I said? Elwyn's father! An august figure whom I hadn't even met! My tongue clove to the roof of my mouth. But before I could unstick it and wind it round any apologies, he spoke again, this time in a tone of the warmest interest. 'But it's funny you should call him that, he *is* rather a miserable old wretch, isn't he?' And peal after peal of laughter rang down the telephone. I have always loved Mr. Davies from that moment.

The Welsh are by nature exceedingly polite, which can lead to problems. They like it if English people who have come to live in their country try to learn a few words of their language, but they sometimes let you get away with mistakes of grammar or pronunciation because they fear to hurt your feelings by a correction. One man we knew memorised a sentence which, from hearing it so often on the wireless, he assumed meant something in the nature of 'Good afternoon—how's tricks?' He got into the habit of saying it to his Welsh neighbours, and attributed their air of startled puzzlement to natural surprise at hearing him bring it out so colloquially. Until one day one of them said hesitantly 'Tell me, Mr. Blank, what do you mean when you keep saying to me "Good afternoon, here are the news headlines in Welsh"?'

English as we are, and non-Welsh speaking, we can never be completely absorbed into the community. But as the years go by we come to value more and more the human quality of life in rural Wales. The blacksmith did once say to me, 'You're one of us, now, Mrs. Cragoe', and I should like to think it is so. Certainly, when the crunch comes, there is no doubt that my Welsh scion of nurture overcomes my English stock of blood.

In other words, I like Wales to beat England at Rugby.

ELEVEN

SMALLER FRY

The Bible says 'Unto him that hath shall be given', and it certainly works like that on a farm. The question 'what shall we do with the animals when we go on our holidays?' which prevents many people from adding to their domestic pets, is different for a farmer. If you are going to go away, you have to make such tremendous arrangements anyway that a few dozen dogs, cats, goats, ponies, pigeons, rabbits and what have you slung in on the side make very little difference. We almost never all go away together in any case, so when another odd bit of the animal kingdom is added unto us, it is very welcome to stay.

Pigeons have often spent a few weeks with us, presumably in the course of homing training. One handsome brown one arrived one October afternoon at about tea-time. He pecked about on the ground in an exhausted kind of way, and ignored the cats with such naive complacency that eventually we had to pick him up for his own good. Deeming him to be 'in need of care and protection', we put him in an empty hen cage for the night, and after a good feed of layers' mash, he seemed much more sprightly the next day. When we let him out, he summoned enough strength to flutter up to the top of the hen-shed, but it was two or three days before his conscience grew active enough to call him back to his proper duties.

Another rainbow-hued beauty stayed with us for two or three months, and we had quite begun to consider him ours when he disappeared again. The children, with striking originality, named him 'Pidgy', and when you stood in the yard and called him, he would arrive from nowhere with a great clatter of feathers, and alight on a little flat projection of the garage roof. There he would stamp up and down on his little pink feet, waiting for his handful of coarse calf mix to be thrown up to him, and uttering his little sotto-voce proodling noises. We never knew what happened to him. Perhaps he was lonely and went in search of a mate. Or perhaps one of the cats got him, though he was much more wary than the brown pigeon, and I never found any feathers.

For several years we had a tiny flock of outdoor hens. The original one escaped when we were caging a batch of 4,000 white birds. They are much flightier than the brown ones, and a couple of dozen always used to manage to get away between the lorry and the cages. We used to have quite exciting hen-hunts at first, cornering them in barns and cowsheds, and seizing a fleeing leg in Welsh-style rugby tackle. But this particular hen evaded all our efforts with such skill and persistence that eventually we decided to let her stay free, and take her chance with the foxes. Somehow she acquired the name of Letty Took, and for years she was constantly to be seen about the yards and sheds.

One reason for her long life was that she soon learned to fly up to a high beam in the cowshed to roost for the night, so keeping herself out of the way of prowling predators. The beam she chose ran directly across the milking parlour, and being an early bedder, she was usually comfortably installed before the evening milking began. Thence, like the Lord, she would rain not only upon the just and the unjust, but on all the milking machines, parlour fixtures, and the outsides of the big milk collecting jars. We used to have to put split paper cakebags over them to protect them from Letty's abundance, or they soon began to look like old-fashioned pictures of Christmas puddings, which would not have pleased the Dairy Officer on his round of inspection.

Letty lived alone for about a year before being joined by two other white hens that somehow got out of the hen-shed. Battery hens grow rather long claws, and look altogether duller and paler than outdoor ones, so at first it was easy to see which was which. But as the others wore their claws down by scratching and grew new, tight, glossy coats of feathers and brilliant scarlet combs, you could hardly tell one from another. We called them Tilly Took and Nellie Took, but they never attained quite the individuality of the original Letty.

The cats were not pleased by this access of strength in the outdoor hen department because the hens soon developed a totally unexpected craving for milk. After all the milk has been pumped into the bulk tank, at the end of the milking, you open a tap in the bottom of the collecting jar, and a pint or two dribbles out. This is collected in a dish, and is a traditional farm cat's perquisite, eagerly awaited, morning and evening. But the hens, strutting about the dairy in their overweening boldness, sampled the milk and decided that they liked it. At first the cats tried to share, and there were a few days when they all clustered round the dish together like an illustration in a child's picture book. But, confidence increasing, the hens began to rain vicious pecks on the competition, and although we had about ten cats at that time, not one would stand up to them. I used to think it was the strangest, most unnatural sight in the world to see those three bright-eyed, long-legged hens, leisurely sipping from the pie dish of milk while ten hungry, frustrated cats sat round in a circle, just out of beak-range, balefully waiting for them to finish. The hens didn't actually drink much, but as a matter of principle, they insisted on having first turn.

All three outdoor hens laid splendidly, but they had a tiresome habit of changing their nesting-sites, and several large clutches of eggs were only discovered after they had been abandoned and gone bad. It didn't really matter, because they never cost us anything. They picked up a lot of food scratching around, and always ate any crumbs of cattle cake dropped by the cows. Any little spaces could be filled in by a visit to the food hopper outside the hen-shed, where they shared the spillage with flocks of sparrows, dunnocks, and chaffinches.

In summer they were always up and off their beam before milking began, but of course in winter it was still dark when we started. Switching on the electric lights wakened them up and made them chatty, but it took real morning light looking in at the windows to make them take the plunge into the big world. They always took several minutes to make up their minds for take-off, during which time they would shuffle up and down the beam defecating nervously, and filling the air with their querulous cries. Finally, with a frenzied shriek, one would launch herself into the air and come flapping and planing down to land on the backs or under the feet of the cows waiting in the collecting yard. You never knew quite where they were going to hit; it could be quite nerve-racking, and I have often had a nervous heifer kick her unit off in panic as a screaming white cannon-ball ricocheted past her ear or burst in a flurry of feathers at her feet.

One morning, Letty seemed peculiarly unwilling to get up. She sat up on the beam long after her sidekicks had taken the plunge, making harsh and discordant noises, rather as if someone was tearing a very bad-tempered bit of calico in half. We wondered if anything terrible was wrong with her, but it turned out to be just the prelude to a bout of broodiness. When she did eventually get up at about half past ten, she took herself off to her current nest on top of the hay in the Dutch barn, and with brief excursions for food and water, there she stayed for the next six weeks. White hens of the modern hybrid strains are supposed to have had the instinct for broodiness bred out of them, but all of ours—for they all went broody within a month—were as conscientious as they could possibly be, and sat as tight as wax. As there was no cockerel running with them, their efforts were in vain, although they all sat far longer than the regulation three weeks, the normal time for hatching a fertile hen's egg. I found it a little pathetic. It was interesting to see how exceedingly unobtrusive these snowy-white birds managed to make themselves while they were sitting. Normally tall and slim, in build, they looked almost two-dimensional when they sank into their hollowed-out nests, with heads pulled right back into their shoulders, and eyes hooded. A sitting bird, by a gracious dispensation of providence, has very little scent, and none of our hens was taken by a fox during the long sitting period.

When Letty was quite old, she did briefly choose another roosting site; perhaps she was beginning to find the long journey up to the beam too much for her, although it was always accomplished in stages—floor to parlour gate, gate to cake-hopper, hopper to beam. Whatever the reason, she abandoned the old beam and took to roosting on a gate that divided off the concreted part of the collecting yard from the part still waiting to be done. I thought it was an unsuitable position, within reach of the cows—I imagined they might push her off her perch—so I moved her a couple of times to a safer place on a ladder against the wall. But each time she scrambled back with such a show of irritable determination that I concluded she must know what she was up to. The cows snuffed at her curiously when they came in, and she ruffled all her feathers up and made a scolding squawk, but they soon stopped taking any notice of her. The milking was going on peacefully enough, and I was about two thirds of the way through, when I heard a most dolorous noise. I looked round, and there was a big black heifer pacing proudly round the collecting yard with Letty in her mouth. She looked like a big black labrador, doing a retrieve, but Letty, slowly flapping her wings, had a terrible expression on her face. I think she was more outraged than hurt, however, for when I made the heifer drop her, her first thought was to preen her plumage. The heifer spent some minutes trying to spit the feathers out of her mouth. Letty went straight back to the beam when she had tidied herself up. Obviously she felt that life at such a low level was not for her.

Some breeds or crosses of poultry are what is called sex-linked, that is, the males and females are of different colours, and this shows up quite clearly even in day-old chicks. Others are not, and their sex has to be determined by a chick-sexer, so that the useless cockerels can be destroyed, and only pullets reared. Chick-sexers work up a considerable speed in their bizarre occupation (one which once beat the panel of *What's my line?* causing a riot of mirth when one of the male panel members asked 'Is it a service? Could you perform this service for me?') and, looking at many thousands in a day, they inevitably make a few mistakes. In a batch of, say, 4,000 pullets there are usually two or three cockerels which you weed out as maturity makes them apparent. An accident of this sort led to the arrival on this farm of Ambrose, the Terror of the West, the bird with the strongest personality I have ever known.

We were caging a load of brown birds, when the man who was catching them from the delivery crates held one up and said 'This one's a cockerel—I'd better pull its neck.' But, thinking of the long, fruitless sittings of the Took family, I said, 'No, let him go—he can live with the outdoor hens and crow to wake us up in the mornings.' 'And that,' as Kipling's Pyecroft once said, 'was my mistake. I should have killed him.'

Ambrose (his full name was Ambrose Applejohn, but he soon declared himself as a character with no need of a surname) started quietly. He skulked in the haybarn for a couple of days, making cautious sorties to the food and water I put out for him, but darting nervously behind a bale if any of his mistresses came into view. He didn't seem to know the rudiments of husbandry, so to speak, and his crowing was the non-event of the year. Mostly he was silent, but if moved to great panic by a terrible experience like seeing a passing dragonfly, or the shadow of a bird's wing, he made the noise a hen makes when it has laid an egg. We feared for his virility, but made allowances for him, considering the largely feminine environment he had been brought up in. As it turned out, we need not have worried.

After a few days he began to associate with the hens, and soon gained the strength and technique to accompany them up to their beam at nights. He grew almost while we watched him, and became a tall arrogant creature, red-feathered, with a great green-black plume of a tail, enormous dangling blood-red wattles, and a mad orange eye. Crowing came next, and when he had mastered it, he practised early and late, until the valley rang with his efforts, and other cocks, as far away as Pant and Rhosyn Goch felt constrained to answer him. By now he was a classic Miltonian figure:

> While the cock, with lively din
> Scatters the rear of darkness thin,
> And to the stack or the barn door
> Stoutly struts his dames before,

and if he had stopped there, it would have been all right, but he continued to grow in ungodliness. His first act of aggression, basely enough, was against a visiting child. Her mother, a friend of mine, had dropped in, and we were chatting in the front yard. Victoria had wandered away behind the buildings, but in a few minutes she came running back, crying, with quite a cut on her leg, where, she said, a 'nasty hen' had pecked her.

Soon our own children were complaining that he was attacking them, but as they were bigger, and usually wearing wellingtons, there was no actual bodily harm. We still cherished the illusion that Ambrose could be taught his place by a show of firmness, and we incited them to retaliate when he came at them. 'Shout!' we told them. 'Clap! Wave your arms! Kick him in the teeth!' But Ambrose was already tough, and this treatment only developed his cunning.

Eventually he turned his aggression on Desmond and me, and became absolutely dauntless. His method was to approach from behind, and launch himself silently into the air when he was within about a yard of you. He would arrive, a flapping, pecking, striking tornado—he always stuck his claws out in front as he attacked—at about the back of your knees, and although he never actually inflicted a wound through our boots and trousers, it was sometimes quite alarming. We have to carry stacks of eggs round from the hen-shed to the grading rooms, and we found ourselves keeping a very keen ear open for the slap-slap of Ambrose's feet on the concrete while we were doing this job. The way to send him off was to launch a vigorous counter-attack, with imprecations, kicks, blows, and stone-throwing, and fifteen dozen eggs in your hands inhibits you comprehensively for counter-attacking.

Above all, Ambrose's nastiness used to make me feel so outraged. Who in hell did he think he was, anyway? People told us that the way to cut him down to size was to give him a real blasting, 'teach him who's the boss', so we decided to do this, and Desmond armed himself with a long-handled muck-fork, and went round the back of the cowshed to teach him the facts of life. He did not have to wait for a confrontation. Merely to set foot in that yard was regarded by Ambrose as an act of provocation, and now he flew at Desmond, eyes glaring wildly, spurs at the ready, and wattles suffused with rage. But Desmond was ready, and as Ambrose launched himself forward, knocked the feet from under him with a sweeping blow of the fork. Ambrose was sent scuttering across the road on his regal beam-end. He was furious. With a screaming crow, he recovered himself, and rushed at his adversary. But this time as he hurled himself into the air, Desmond caught him a giant thwack across the side with the flat of the fork, that sent him spinning into the cowshed wall. He dropped to the ground and lay motionless, with all the breath knocked out of him. 'Christ, I've killed him,' thought Desmond, hurrying up to look. But as he approached, the inert bundle of feathers raised its head and crowed, twice, defiantly, lying there on the ground. Then he scrambled shakily to his feet and tottered up the yard, supporting himself against the cowshed wall, and crowing fiercely at every second step. He turned into the dark doorway, and bundled himself into a corner. Thinking that if he was too much damaged, he would have to be bumped off, Desmond left him alone for an hour to sort himself out. But when egg-carrying time came round, there he was, a little stiff, a little slow off the mark, but distinctly unbowed. He attacked Desmond as per schedule. Matthew, who was in a soccer phase, said we should display warning notices saying 'Ambrose pecks yer legs'.

Another hate of Ambrose's was the tractor. Presumably its bigness and redness struck him as potentially inimical; at any rate, he used to expend himself in a frenzy of pecks and scratches at the front wheels when it began to move, and always crowed in a self-congratulatory way as it disappeared round the corner.

His most nearly successful attack was aimed at my very tall cousin, Bruce. He was just going into the hen-shed when Ambrose decided that his presence could no longer be tolerated, and sailed in to liquidate him. Unfortunately for Bruce, Ambrose was standing at the top of the cleaning-out ramp at the time, so instead of attacking Bruce's calves, he arrived, kicking and screaming, just below his face. 'It was quite frightening,' Bruce told us. 'He looker enormous, and somehow prehistoric. It was like being attacked by a pterodactyl.' We discussed the possibility of Ambrose having used the advantage of the ramp on purpose, or at least, of his learning from it as a fortunate accident. Having a foul-tempered cockerel at ground level was bad enough; receiving him regularly at face level, perhaps with one's hands full of egg trays, was impossible to contemplate. We decided to dispose of him.

But this was not the end of the road for Ambrose. Welshmen notoriously admire tough fighters, and by now his fame as the most horrible cockerel ever to crack an egg had spread throughout the district. A farmer from the Llanelli area, a friend of a friend, had heard of him, and, wanting a cockerel to run with his fifteen farmyard hens, offered to take him off our hands. Catching him was not without anxiety, for he had a peck like the hammer of God, but we took him unexpectedly with a torch in the dark after he had gone to roost—luckily not on the beam for once. Our last view of him was as he lay, legs bound, eyes glaring, on the back seat of the car, carefully draped for the occasion with split paper feed bags.

For several months we had reports of his progress, which we had to pass on to all those of our friends and relations who, having suffered from his attentions, still took an interest in him. Fifteen wives proving insufficiently quenching for him, his new owner eased the number up to twenty-seven. Here a balance was struck; Ambrose still attacked everything and everybody, but perfunctorily—his energies were obviously being put to a better use. There was a certain anxiety lest he should attack the farmer's eighty-year-old mother, but the sheep-dog kept him down at his own end of the yard, away from the house, and for a few months all was well.

But fate could not run smoothly for long for a character cast in Ambrose's craggy mould. One day the sheep-dog ran on to the road in front of a car and was killed. Without its disciplinary influence, Ambrose began to include more and more of the yard in his territory. Within a few weeks, the poor old lady dared not set foot outside her own kitchen door for fear of his sharp disapproval. So in the end he had to be executed, and made, I believe, quite a tasty meal, after long boiling.

The outdoor hens no longer roam the yard. Letty sickened and died when quite an old hen of four, and the other two, with a brown one who had joined them, developed a rogue appetite for eggs. We were storing the eggs in the old cowshed at the time, and these wretched birds began to eat them. They would jump on top of a stack of trays and scratch vigorously. Eggs would fly off in all directions, breaking all over the floor, and the pirates would settle down to a pleasant meal. Had they confined their depredations to an egg or two a day we should probably never have noticed, but when we discovered one morning that the three of them had broken nineteen in the half hour between getting up and breakfast, it was the end. Desmond wrung their necks, but although we plucked and dressed the anonymous brown one, we couldn't bring ourselves to eat the mortal remains of Tilly and Nellie. I suppose they were tidied away by the cats.

There are people who have been heard to say that there is a bit too much cat about this farm. I could never think so. Our present establishment is nine permanent cats, and one constant visitor, but this is necessarily a fluid figure. Kittens are born, cats are killed on the road—sometimes we give a kitten away. But there are always plenty of friendly furry faces around. It is one of my greatest pleasures to look through the glass door of the kitchen and see the line-up of classic features, all marked in the same pattern, all ready to burst out purring at the touch of a hand.

Our present line of cats began when Dai came to work for us, The cat that arrived in Wales with us was Mitten, a neutered seal-point male Siamese. He liked the farm, but with his urban background he never quite, we felt, moulded into the country scene. We felt the need of cats around the place that would be happy in the barns and sheds, and would also catch mice. Mitten, albeit charming, had a decided squint which seemed to inhibit his pursuit of prey. He just didn't seem able to judge the distances right. Sometimes he didn't even try. One evening we were sitting round the fire in the kitchen when a mouse emerged from a hole beside the fireplace. It walked into the middle of the floor, where it stopped and consumed a small fragment of toast. Then, pausing only to clean its whiskers, it ambled over to the diagonally opposite corner of the room and squeezed its fat person into another mousehole there. Mitten watched it benevolently.

So when Dai came to us, we asked him if he could get us a kitten or two from somewhere. 'Kittens?' said Dai. 'I can get you kittens, easy. Bloody hundreds, man.' The first of the hundreds was a little female cat that had been eking out a precarious life as a stray in the village for eighteen months or so. Tiny and stunted her fur was tortoise-shell, with large areas of white and patterned patches of orange and grey. Huge green eyes burned in a little pointed face. We called her Tippin Bach—Welsh for a little bit—Tippin for short. Tippin couldn't believe her luck at being somebody's cat at last. She ate everything we put in front of her, and although she was long past kittenhood, I am sure she grew a little. She was a most affectionate cat, and loved to follow us round the farm as we went about our work. She would balance along the concrete stall partitions as I gave hay and cake to the young heifers; her eyes would glow in the shadows, and her hoarse, vibrant purr would make the very cobwebs tremble.

We very much hoped that she would have kittens, but no tomcat suitor ever seemed to be present, and we wondered if perhaps her early stunting when she was a stray had made her infertile. Or it might be, we thought, that no farm near us happened to have a tomcat at the time. Dai offered to cut this Gordian knot by bringing his mother's cat Thomas to visit us for a few weeks. 'He's a lovely cat,' he told us, 'all black, and a proper cwrcyn too—great big broad head on him.' (Cwrcyn, pronounced coorkin, is Welsh for tomcat.)

So Thomas the cwrcyn was brought, and shut up in the stable with his intended lady-love. But as a love-match it seemed doomed to failure. Thomas, released, rushed into the darkest corner of the manger, where he crouched, trembling. Tippin leapt up the ladder and went to ground in an overturned eggbox in the loft. Considering that propinquity might be the best medicine, we left food, milk and water available, shut the door, and went to do the evening milking.

We had intended to leave them together in the bridal suite for several days, until Thomas got used to his new situation and began to feel at home; but next morning when we opened the door, only Tippin emerged, tail erect, wreathed in purrs. Tom Cwrcyn was not there. Doors, windows, were all shut fast; but somehow, like a genie, he had made himself small and squeezed through an impossible crack. 'He will have gone home,' said Dai confidently, and as Oernant is only a mile and a half away, upwind and clearly visible from our farm, this seemed the most likely outcome. But as day followed day, and Thomas didn't turn up, we all felt worse and worse. Gloomily, we discussed the possibilities. He might have been killed on the road and his body flung over a hedge; he might have been caught and sold to the vivisection people (unlikely, this, as he was too nervous to be easily picked up by a stranger). Or, most likely, he might be lurking round the countryside, helpless and lost, with no idea why his own peaceful, well-known farmyard had so suddenly vanished. He was not a very bright cat. We all felt very sorry for our part in his misfortunes, and we hunted for him early and late all over the farm and in our neighbours' fields, but in vain.

But one day, about three weeks after his unscheduled departure, Dai was walking from the stable to the hen-shed, when he thought he heard a tiny mew. It came from a big clump of nettles, and when he parted them and looked in, there was Thomas. He was lured out with a saucer of milk, and when he had drunk it, he looked up at Dai with a deprecating glance, as if to say 'The world is a bit too big for me—pray take me back to my own home!' So Dai took him back there and then, to his mother's great joy and contentment. Thomas soon recovered his portly figure, and lives in Oernant to this day; but whether or not he ever boasts to the other cats about his exotic experiences as a stud tom, there is no means of telling.

Tippin duly became pregnant, but shortly before she was due to have her kittens, she was killed on the road. We buried her in the garden, glad that at least her death had been instant.

Dai, who had been looking forward to the arrival of the kittens as eagerly as any of us, began enquiring round for another cat, and before long he had located two female kittens belonging to a barn cat on the farm of an elderly widow near Oernant. He said he would bring them back after his next visit home. In the event they proved so difficult to catch that he brought them one at a time, in a sack. The first to arrive was a neat little black and white with strikingly symmetrical markings. Bars of darker

colour showed in the black parts of her coat, and for this reason
we christened her Shadow. Decanted from her sack onto the
kitchen floor, she ignored the saucers of milk and food that we
had put out, and streaked, belly to earth, behind the refrigerator.
Trying to squeeze underneath it for greater security, she managed
to get herself stuck, and we had to prise the front off the bottom
bit to get her out. Gently I pulled her free and stroked her, but
she was terrified, and I could feel her rigid little body trembling
under my hand. As soon as we let her go, she rushed behind the
refrigerator again.

So when the other kitten arrived the next evening, we
decided to adventure the pair of them in the stable. We made
the door a tighter fit, and put several boxes and heaps of hay for
them to hide in; at least, we thought, it wouldn't be quite so
traumatic for them as constantly getting stuck under the refrigerator.

For the first week, the kittens were totally wild, and rushed
out of sight at the rattle of the door-latch. Then they began to
associate my visits with the replenishment of food-dishes, and I
would see their little triangular faces peeping cautiously round
stall partitions, or through the loft trapdoor. By the third week,
they ventured to feed in my presence, as long as I sat very still.
They were still extremely nervous, though, and the slightest
movement on my part would send them scuttling away into the
straw. The next stage was to hold the saucers full of food on my
lap, as I sat on the floor, so that they had to climb partly on to my
knee to get their food. Then they had to endure my touching
them while they ate; but from then on, progress was quick, and
they soon learned to welcome, not merely to endure, the touch of
the human hand. The second kitten, slightly larger than her sister, was a mackerel tabby with a lot of white on her paws, chest
and face. We called her Silver, and she became the mother of the
line of cats that we still have.

We are now in the seventh generation, although we have been
a little unlucky with females for the past two years, losing in turn
Lutra and Vixen on the road, either of whom would have been
a mother of eighth generation kittens. The pedigree reads rather
like a list of the 'begats' in the Bible, although, unsemitically,
we trace the line of descent through the female parent. Thus,
Silver had Pewter, Pewter had Tunku (named before her sex was
apparent, much to my father's outrage. 'Elizabeth,' he said, 'you

simply *can't* have a pregnant Tunku. It's not done. It's biologically impossible. It's out of the question.') Tunku had Sailor, Sailor had Miss Moppet, Miss Moppet had Badger, and Badger had Lutra and Vixen. We have kept many male kittens as well which, like Fitzgerald's sultans, 'abode their little hour and went their way.'

There was Rumpelstiltskin, inevitably known as Rumpy, one of the sweetest cats we have ever owned. His hunting territory was the hedgebank running down to the Dip field, and whenever you walked that way, he would come hastening out of some lair, waving his tail and purring effusively. He particularly loved ginger cake, and would sit on my shoulder eating it and almost choking with purrs, while I fetched up the cows for milking, then when it was finished, he would gaze deep into my eyes, kneading his claws into the shoulder of my anorak, and breathing scented purrs into my face.

All our cats for many generations have been striped, or even perhaps more spotted, with pale gold-green eyes—eyes that have the same shifts of colour as newly-made rush matting, the same subtle paleness as bales of tribute silk. The patterning on the tops of their heads is intricate, like a Persian carpet, or the markings of a snake; and the backs of their ears are delicately graded in tender tones of hazel. They are extremely close-coated, with a dense, plushy fur that glows with good living. With mice galore, plenty of broken eggs, hens' innards twice a week before market days, and the first pick at any hens that die in the hen-sheds, this place is a paradise of first-class protein for a cat.

Although they make good mothers when they get the idea, our cats have always been casual in the extreme about preparing for their kittens. Silver was the first to kitten with us, and she was taken completely flat aback by the whole business. We had a fireplace in the kitchen in those days, and we were all sitting peacefully around it one evening. Silver was lying on the rush matting at our feet, when she suddenly shot straight up into the air and emitted a piercing yowl. Coming down to earth again, she hastily sat down and shoved a back leg up over her shoulder. In this position she stared disbelievingly at her nether end, from which, sure enough, the head of a kitten was protruding. Fair play to her, once she had accepted the situation she managed very nicely, and the other kittens were duly born and reared in the cardboard box we found for her.

130

Pewter was one of these kittens, and she inherited in full strength her mother's come-day-go-day attitude to family responsibilities. She also produced her young in the evening, actually while I was trying to listen to *Coronation Street*. The children, ready for bed, were sitting by the fire, and I couldn't understand why they were making such an irritating noise. 'Do stop making that stupid squeaking' I said, rather crossly. 'I'm trying to listen to this programme.' 'It isn't us,' they said, all injured innocence, and then Rachel noticed it. 'Look!' she cried. 'It's a kitten! Over on the floor by the television set!' We put it into a box, and added Pewter, who was casually washing herself in another part of the kitchen, taking no notice of its cries. Strangely, as soon as she was in the box with it, she began to look after it, and remained a most conscientious mother until it was grown up. Neither Silver nor Pewter ever had any other litters, as we had them neutered as soon as we were sure they had produced a female kitten. Tunku was Pewter's only offering; presumably any other kittens of the litter must have been dropped in the same casual way, but outside. At any rate, we never found them.

Sailor was the most wayward of our cats, a fact that nearly cost one of her kittens its life. She had a litter or two in a nest in the stable, close to the stack of cattle cake, which was in fifty-six pound bags. Before starting milking in the evening, Desmond would carry over enough of these bags for a day's requirements, and empty them into the two cake-hoppers in the milking parlour. Now these hoppers were Sailor's idea of a perfect place for her kittens, and about five times a week she would carry them there, jump six feet up the sheer outside elevation, and deposit them therein on top of the knobbly cake. Sometimes they were together—sometimes there was one in each hopper. We used to fish them out and return them to their proper place when we got the parlour ready for evening milking.

One day, being in a hurry, Desmond tipped in the first bag of cake without thinking of the kittens, and went back for a second. Luckily his eye was caught by a squirming movement in the nest beside the bag-stack, and he suddenly registered with horror that there was only one kitten there. We rushed back to the parlour —looked in the empty hopper—no kitten! It must be in the other hopper under fifty-six pounds of cattle cake! Frantically, we dug around with our hands, and almost immediately, my fingers closed around a little limp body. I fished it out and laid it, pathetically flat, on the palm of my hand. It looked utterly crushed—it had to be dead after such an experience, but suddenly, against all expectation, it stirred, sneezed, and before our very eyes, miraculously re-inflated. We popped it hastily back with its sibling, and their screw-brained Mamma, and by the evening of the next day there was nothing to show which kitten it had been. Those kittens grew up to be Rumpelstiltskin and Miss Moppet, neither of whom was in any way remarkable for flatness.

The flattest cat we ever had was called Shamouti. He made the fatal error of creeping right into one of a stack of empty paper cake-bags in the meal-room, and curling up for a sleep. Desmond, staggering in with a hundredweight sack of sugar beet pulp, dropped it on top of him without realising he was there. He looked like an opera hat when we found him. Poor Shamouti! At least I think his death must have been very quick. His brother, Scipio, was a beautiful cat. We had heavy snow in the winter when he was about eight months old, and he went nearly mad with excitement when he saw it. He played in it, like a child, until he was quite exhausted. He looked so oriental, with his bushed-out tail, big theatrical snarl, and wide-spread dragon claws as he skittered sideways across the yard that his name somehow got changed to China Tiger, or China for short.

People say 'Give a dog a bad name and hang him'; only once have we given a cat one, and he certainly came to a sticky end. He was a big, dark, neutered tomcat originally called Sable, because of the heavy black stripes down his back. But my father, who had been re-reading Bunyan's *Life and Death of Mr. Badman*, remarked one day that it sounded like the biography of a cat, and somehow, imperceptibly, it came to be Sable's pet-name.

At that time we were rearing chickens from the day-old stage to dress for the table at ten to twelve weeks old. Occasionally, one died, but you expect a few losses in a batch of chicks, and at first the odd corpse in the six-week-old batch did not seem particularly sinister. True, each one was picked to a skeleton when we found it, but might not that be a rogue rat, eating an already dead bird? We put bait down, and kept our eyes open. But the losses continued, and finally the ill-named Mr. Badman was caught in the very act. It was rather tragic, because we were fond of him, but there seemed no alternative to execution. There was no way of keeping him out of the poultry pens, and we felt that he was too old a cat to settle happily in a new home, even if we had been able to find one for him. So he got the needle. Luckily no other cat even looked at the rearing chickens, and as we no longer keep them now, none ever will.

Our youngest current cats are a charming pair of heavenly twins called Castor and Pollux. Their mother, Badger, has been one of our most successful mothers until recently, but her last litter was a fiasco. It was the next litter after the Castor and Pollux lot, and was born during the very hot summer of 1975. By a dreadful error of judgement, Badger elected to have it in the egg packing room, and, having hidden in there when the door was locked for the night, found her way into a butter box that still had three pounds of butter in it. The resultant hollandaise almost defied description. The heat of her body melted the butter, and when we found her in the morning she looked like a drowned rat. Every hair on her tail, her legs, and the underside of her body, was dripping with melted butter—the kittens were swimming in it—everything was awash. Usually so loving and sweet with her kittens, she had not touched these—they were already chilled and dying, and even when we put them, mopped up, into a clean box, she simply didn't want to know them. They had to be destroyed in the end. Presumably her sense of smell must have been stifled by the excess of butter, and the particular scent-message that usually triggers off the appropriate behaviour-pattern, had been thwarted. We washed off what we could of her unwelcome dressing, but it was three days before her coat fluffed out properly again. Then she settled down in a happy family group with her six-month-old kittens, who were delighted to have a second period of nursing, and nobody seemed to miss the kittens *au beurre* at all.

TWELVE

ENTER THE WELSH BLACKS

In the summer of 1973 we came to a decision that altered our way of farming fundamentally. We decided to give up dairying. For some years, its profits had been showing up badly in the farm books in comparison with the poultry business. It was dirty; I was the milker, and not being very good at remembering to put my overall on, I kept getting muck on my clothes. I didn't mind it, but people not constantly handling cows found me smelly. And it was very tying. With hens you can, at a pinch, feed them in the morning and leave them for twenty-four hours. Everything they need—lighting, water, and ventilation, is automatic. But with dairy cows there has to be twice-a-day attendance, preferably at the exact twelve-hour interval, from somebody who knows which one is which. You can put identification marks on them, like numbered neckbands, heelstraps, or freeze brands, which show up as white numbers in the black bits of their coats, but we never got around to this. We knew the cows ourselves, and on the few occasions when we had to miss a milking and Dai milked for us, we worked out a simple code to show each animal's cake ration—a figure, in eyebrow pencil, denoting pounds of cake, on a white bit of the rump, and a big red cross with a cattle-marking stick on the dry cows.

We had some disappointments, too. After years of bull-calves, Candytuft, the best cow we ever had, brought us a heifer whose father was a particularly fashionable bull called Tredene Jan Alidema. We cherished it and it grew in grace until it was a fine strapping bulling heifer, when it was duly put in calf. We awaited its accouchement and graduation into the milking herd with bated breath.

As the calving date drew nearer, a beautiful little udder began to form. I fed Candytuft Junior a ration of cake every evening in the milking-parlour, and while she was eating it, rubbed and handled her udder so that the putting on of the milking machine

134

should not cause her too much outrage. Candy quite enjoyed these attentions, and usually pushed her way well to the front of the queue the sooner to get at her meal. But one evening, a day or two before she was due, I noticed that she came last as the cows filed into the collecting yard, and seemed to straddle her back legs a little as she walked along. She ate her cake, however, and though her bag felt a little tense to my fingers, I thought it was only the firmness that comes when the udder begins to fill, just before calving.

The strange walking was even more pronounced the next morning, and we began to worry. We called the vet and told him we thought one of our down-calving heifers was suffering from pre-calving fever, but he scouted that idea straight away. 'It can't be milk fever in a heifer,' he said. 'They never have it. I'd better come up and have a look at her.'

Vets are cheerful souls as a rule, but this one's face was grave as he looked at our heifer. He took her temperature, and we were shocked to find it was 105°F. He passed a hand over her udder, and drew a sample of milk from each of her teats. Three of them yielded thick, creamy colostrum, but from the fourth all he could wring, with difficulty, was a little clear, serous fluid, slightly bloodstained.

'Your heifer has black garget, I'm afraid,' he told us. 'And I don't like the look of that quarter at all.' 'What are the chances of saving it?' we asked, shaken. 'The quarter? Absolutely nil, I'd say. We'll have enough job to save the heifer. This is a systematic infection now—you've got a very sick beast on your hands.' And after injecting her and advising us about nursing care, he left, promising to call back the next day.

We did save the heifer, but the quarter, as predicted, was ruined. She calved a few days later, producing from her three good quarters just enough milk to feed the little thing, instead of the four or five gallons we had anticipated. Eventually the affected quarter sloughed right off, and when she had healed up and put back, by six months' grazing, the weight she lost in her illness, we had to send her to the . . . mart.

You don't, of course, change your farming policy over one heifer; rather, it was a last straw. The Government were offering a substantial grant at the time to dairy farmers to persuade them to change over to beef cattle, and, after talking it over carefully, we decided to take the plunge.

This meant having a farm sale to get rid of our Friesians. We could have taken them to the market one by one as they calved, but having decided to break with dairying, we wanted to get on and get it done, and selling them on the farm seemed the best plan.

I was surprised by the amount of organisation that it took to sell about forty cows and heifers. The auctioneers were marvellous, but as many of our cows were pedigree, and milk recorded, it was decided to produce a catalogue, and of course only we could do that. I struggled through years of figures; the man who is paying a good price for a pedigree animal likes to know not only how much milk she has produced in all her lactations, but also the figures for her dam, grandam, and sire's dam. Butterfat percentages too must be included, and the number of days each lactation has lasted. A separate section on bulls used in the herd gives the yields of both their ancestors and their progeny—their sires' unselected daughters' average yields, ditto for their dam's sire—even the colour of their second cousins' tails, I felt might be asked for, after a week or two of compiling. Desmond wrote an introduction for the catalogue, which briefly outlined our source material for the herd and our policy in the selection of sires.

One advantage of selling by catalogue, and emphasising the pedigree part of the herd was that pedigree cattle are always sold in guineas rather than pounds, and of course the odd shillings are the auctioneers' commission ready-made, so to speak.

A myriad other details had to be settled besides the catalogue. The order in which the cattle were to come into the ring—which building they were to come out of, and which to disappear into after their brief appearance—where was the auctioneer to have his rostrum; who was to do the catering?

Then the cattle themselves had to be given a beauty treatment for their big day, and a team of friends and neighbours washed, clipped, and powdered in the parlour, while Desmond and I ran round in ever-decreasing circles, spreading straw, sticking on numbers, and generally getting in each other's way.

The sale was held on 30 November, and our hopes of a fine day were dashed as soon as we got up. A bone-aching wind snarled up the yard bearing a thick freezing drizzle. A few people rolled up—too few by far, we thought; plenty of them, you could guarantee, were there to watch rather than to buy. But our neighbours were comforting. 'On a day like this, only the ones who are going to bid will have turned out,' opined Howell. 'And they're the ones you want. A big crowd doesn't have to mean a good sale.'

The auctioneer came out of the house, where he had been pressing himself up to the Aga. He rubbed his hands together. 'I'm going to start now, I think,' he said. 'I've given them half an hour after the advertised time. I should think they've come now if they're coming.' So a clerk went round ringing a handbell, the auctioneer climbed onto his rostrum, coughed, and adjusted his microphone; the people formed a ring, and the first animals were driven in. The sale was on!

The first pair in the ring were a newly-calved heifer and her calf. It was a heifer calf, about a fortnight old, a fine upstanding creature with a lot of white about it, and with the toy-shop fresh look that all young calves have. It was offered first.

The bidding began slowly. 'What am I offered for this calf? Fifty? Forty-five? Surely forty? Come, come gentlemen! This is a beautiful calf. Well, I'm in your hands. Start me, somebody. Anywhere you like. Put her in. Bid me, bid me then for this fine heifer calf. Twenty! I've got twenty! Five! Thirty! Thirty! Five! Forty! Five! Forty-five guineas for this lovely little heifer! And she looks a good one! Fill her up, gentlemen! Can I go fifty? Fifty I've got! Any more? and five! Fifty-five guineas! It's against you sir—you're in at the back! Will you come again? Sixty? You lose her—sixty, sixty——' and so on, until the first hammer crashed at seventy-eight. We wiped sweaty hands down the seams of our trousers, and relaxed a little. Seventy-eight guineas was a good price in a falling market.

Beast after beast was driven out, praised, moved round the ring, and sold. Some prices were good, some fair, one or two lamentable. But at the end of the day we were well content with a top price of 300 guineas and a fair few others not too far behind it. And when the last beast had been driven up the ramp of the last lorry we felt a strange lightness as we surveyed the debris. Everything was in a revolting mess, with the trampled sodden straw of the ring, abandoned catalogues flapping, and the caterer's cardboard cups blowing up and down the yard, but for the first time in nine years there was no evening milking to do. For good or ill, the die was cast. We were out of milk.

Under the Government scheme, the 'golden handshake' as it

137

was called, we had to replace the cattle with an equal number of units of a beef breed. Calculation of units was complex; but what it came down to in hard facts was that we had to acquire thirty-one breeding females and a bull.

We had no difficulty in choosing a breed. I had happy childhood memories of the Welsh Black cattle on Gwill's farm in Dolgellau; true, in those days they were run as a milking herd, but that was thirty years ago. Now the Welsh Black is recognised as one of the most useful single suckling breeds, where each cow rears her own calf, producing a fine big yearling to sell on to a fattener at the end of the season. The Welsh Black is a hardy animal, and an outstandingly good forager; she is really bred for worse land than ours, but for once we listened to the dictates of fancy rather than those of pure business, and, turning our back on the lush pastures of Hereford or Devon, went up the lovely coast road to Dolgellau to see what we could do for ourselves.

The Farmers' Mart at Dolgellau looked funny to our eyes, long acquainted with the hornless, boldly-patterned Friesians of milder climes. It was November when we made our first sally, so the animals were in their winter coat, and when a Welsh Black grows a winter coat, she is clearly preparing for the worst that nature can throw at her. With thick black fur, two or three inches long, often curly, the animals stood in their market stalls like so many teddy bears, or moved uneasily in the larger pens, clashing their fine spreading horns against one another. The eye, accustomed to assessing the conformation of a milker, the famous 'dairy wedge', had to come to terms with a new set of standards. A good beef beast is described not as a 'wedge', but 'as an evenly fleshed block of meat on four short legs'. I, as usual, was distracted by curly coats, shapely horns and wistful dark eyes; but Desmond's objectivity triumphed, and at the end of the day we had twenty-two fine bulling heifers to get home somehow.

Getting beasts home from your local market, or farm sales in your own district is quite easy. You know all the hauliers, and besides, they are all there. The lorry park at the market is full of familiar vehicles, so if you can't actually waylay the driver you want, you can leave a note on his lorry, and know that sooner or later that day your animals will arrive. But when you are a hundred miles from home you are out of your territory. We failed to find a Dolgellau lorry willing to set off on the perilous route south at that time in the evening, and eventually our own Carmarthen man brought up his big lorry for them. They arrived home at about midnight, and we shepherded them down the ramp and into the covered yard to eat hay, and rest, after what must have been a very long and trying day for them.

It was at this point that we made a most stupid mistake, the effects of which are still with us. Friesian cattle, with their bold magpie markings, are as individual as fingerprints, and when we bought several at a time we used to write their names on a white bit in eyebrow pencil, and know them by the time the names washed off. But all-over blackness is one of the essential desiderata of a Welsh Black; a little white on the udder, though frowned upon, is not precluded; anyone who takes an eyebrow pencil to the udder of a mountain-reared bulling heifer, however, must answer for some pretty explosive consequences—as a means of identification, it didn't recommend itself. The official identification is a tattoo in the right ear, but you can only see this by getting the animal tied up or in a cattle crush, seizing its ear, turning it inside out, and clawing away the plentiful black hair of the lining—to all of which the animal objects as strenuously as it knows how. What we should have done was to put some field mark, like a coloured neck-band with numbers on it, on them, while they still had their sale numbers pasted on their rumps. It would have been an easy and painless way, and we should soon enough have got to recognise them as individuals. But what we did was nothing, and when the animals went out in the field and the rain washed the numbers off their rumps, we couldn't tell t'other from which. We were, it is true, preoccupied with the arrangements for our own sale at the time, but even so it was stupid of us. The result is that we still don't know more than a handful of them, and every time a calf has to be registered, for instance, we have to catch up the mother and look in her ear to see who she is.

Another factor that made identification difficult was that we decided to have the horns off them. We originally thought to keep them on, because they are so beautiful, but our vet groaned and rolled up his eyes at our folly. 'There's one born every day,' he said. 'These animals can be very nasty when they're protecting a young calf, and you'll be sorry you missed the chance of getting those horns off when you find one of them through your chest one fine day!' So we spent a dreadful blood-battered afternoon with him removing them all, and when the sore places healed up, the cows looked more anonymous than ever. It isn't so much that they are hard to tell apart, as that you never know which name goes with which face.

We decided, as a matter of policy, to spend on Welsh Blacks the money we got for our Friesians. We still had nine young Friesan heifers which we hadn't put in the sale, and one or two old grannies that had failed to reach their reserves; so with the twenty-two heifers, we were technically all right for numbers for the time being. What we needed was a bull, and as about £1,000 remained in the kitty, we felt we could afford a fairly plushy one.

Changing breeds in cattle is rather like going metric in that you have to discard all your preconceived notions, throw out all your comfortable old mental furniture, and acquire a complete new set. After a few years in pedigree Friesians we were familiar with the names of the nationally famous herds, and more familiar with many of the good herds in our own district. Through studying catalogues and talking to breeders you get an outline picture in your mind of a herd—its strengths and weaknesses, any particular blood-lines it breeds to, the type of cattle it favours. You can even sometimes recognise the progeny of a particularly pre-potent bull, a real boost to the ego; you buy cattle, therefore, from a background of information, and for clearly-defined reasons.

Plunging fairly wholesale into the Welsh Black world, we felt the lack of this kind of knowledge. The names in the pedigree catalogues at sales were just names, the famous and the nondescript. Nothing produced the automatic mental genuflexion that the names of, say, Grove or Tesling would in a Friesian sale. And yet it was important for us to know this. In breeding pedigree stock for sale, fashion is just as important as merit, and an indifferent animal of the right breeding may well fetch more money than a glamorous unknown.

What we did for a start was to collect up all the back numbers of the *Farmer's Weekly* that we could find, and study the show reports. We noted the herds that seemed to be consistently successful, and followed up their successes in the reports of autumn sales. If they did well there too we looked them up in the catalogues, and took note also of the herds from which they had bought bulls for their own use. This gave us a list of about ten herds which seemed to be in the money, and we tried to select our stock from animals carrying blood from these herds.

One animal in recent years has dominated the Welsh Black breed to such an extent that his portrait always appears on the cover of the main sale catalogues. This is Chwaen Major 15th, a bull who has more than once been supreme champion over all the beef breeds at the Royal Show. At the time he was standing in a herd called Rhydygarnedd, and we determined, if possible, to have one of his sons for our herd sire.

It was a cold January day when we set off hopefully with our thousand pounds clutched metaphorically in our pockets, to try to get our bull. I was at school in Dolgellau, so I always enjoy a visit there, and even if we didn't get a bull, or the bull we wanted, it would be a lovely day out, I thought, driving up through some of the most beautiful scenery in Wales. The road from Carmarthen hugs the Cardigan coast; you look down steep cliff-edged fields onto the grey, crawling sea. Thrawn, wind-sculptured gorse-bushes line the road, sprinkled with gold even in January; and then comes Aberystwyth with its yacht basin and its huddle of dark slate roofs. From here onward, the earth folds more and more violently, and the scenery is breath-takingly dramatic. We love to drive up in May, when the bluebells stand thickly about the roots of the golden-leaved oaks on rocky knolls in the roadside fields; but I felt in a way that the sombre majesty of this January day was more in keeping with the magnificence of the mountains. Up towered the great slaty peaks, their heads wreathed in cloud, while the shoulders of the foothills glowed in fox-coloured wet bracken or the spicy green of the forestry plantations. Singing brooks, clear as green glass, rushed down the valleys, and the mountains parted, fold on fold, to reveal the gracious distances of the Dovey estuary.

Stiff from travelling, we tumbled out of the car at Dolgellau and went, catalogue in hand, to have a look at the talent. There were four bulls that interested us from their breeding, and two of them were sons of Chwaen Major 15th.

When you intend to spend a fair sum of money it is not unreasonable to put the vendor to a certain amount of trouble, so we looked at these four bulls from all angles. We had them brought out and walked past us, walked towards, walked away, so that we could study their action. They were all weight-recorded (an important factor in a beef animal, where speed of

141

weight gain means an earlier date with the slaughter man and more money in the farmer's pocket), but the one who had done best had something about the set of his hocks that we didn't quite fancy. Another was worrying his stockman because, upset by the strangeness of the journey and the market, he would not eat or drink. 'He looks twice this at home,' he kept saying distressfully, pushing his fists into the sad little creature's flanks. 'Look at those hollows! They'd go right away if he'd just eat his meal. But I can't tempt him! Not a bite or sup has passed his lips since yesterday noon! It's a different taste on the water here, you know.'

In the end we decided that the best bull was the smaller of the Rhydygarnedd ones, but as he was the last of our four fancies to go, it was risky to pin all our hopes on him. 'I may settle for one of the others,' said Desmond. 'They're all nice enough bulls. We'll just have to see how the bidding goes.'

So we settled down in our seats, high up in the crowded amphitheatre, and waited. It was amusing to see how differently the bidding was conducted from Carmarthen market. There the auctioneer pushes business along fairly briskly, and is not above administering a gentle rebuke if he feels the buyers are hanging back on their bids. 'Come along, gentlemen!' he will say. 'We've a lot to get through! I shall sell her! She's in the market to be sold! You're going to lose her if you don't hurry up!' But the Dolgellau auctioneers seemed endlessly indulgent, and the bids were squeezed out in a reluctant, constipated kind of way.

Not so when Desmond started to bid, however. He has never been one to hang about, and, knowing exactly what his top limit was for each bull, he briskly bid it up till he reached it. The old farmers round the ringside were scandalised; who was this barbarian who so airily flouted the tradition of years? Darting glances were cast over weathered shoulders, and you could hear the hissing whisper 'sais!' (English) passing round the ring.

The auctioneers, however, were encouraged, and the vendors delighted. The three bulls of our second choice came to the limits Desmond had set for them, passed it, and were knocked down to their new owners. Quite a hum of conversation rose, and the auctioneer had to bang with his gavel and ask everybody to be quiet.

At last, the little bull of our choice was led in. He had won second prize in his class, and his Cambridge blue rosette nestled

142

against his coal-black curls with an air. He was led round and round, and as the auctioneer expatiated on his breeding, we admired again the straight back, even fleshing and perfect hind legs that had made us choose him in the first place.

The bidding started, and again there was a little rustle of interest when Desmond came in and speeded it up. Six hundred guineas was quickly passed. And fifty! Seven! and fifty! Eight! Our money was in pounds, so we had to do a little ready reckoner on the back of an envelope showing how it converted into guineas. I saw Desmond glancing at it. 'Eight fifty! I'll take ten now, gentlemen!' Up, up, it went, slower now, but inexorably. Somebody down there wanted him as badly as we did. Nine hundred and forty guineas! It was coming near the limit, and it was the last of the bulls we wanted. Desmond played his trump card. The bidding had been rising in tens for some time, but now, as he caught the auctioneer's eye, I saw him nod, and his lips soundlessly framed the word 'twenty'.

'Nine hundred and sixty guineas I am bid! Nine hundred and sixty! Will you take him all the way, Sir? May I say a thousand? No? Then I'm going to sell him! Going! For nine hundred and sixty guineas! Going! Gone!' He was ours.

A glance at the table showed us that he had cost us £1,008, and another twenty had to be added to that to get him home. The Rhydygarnedd family gave us last-minute instructions on his diet, and made us a present of half a bag of the special coarse mix he was accustomed to. 'Eight pounds a day of that he's eating,' they told us. 'And you can use this at first so he won't feel it so strange. Then he can change over to whatever mix you use gradually.'

We put him in the covered yard for an acclimatising period before introducing him to his wives. Elwyn came to see him, and laid a hand on his back. We thought he was feeling the evenness of the fleshing, but he said it was more a gesture of reverence. 'I don't think I've ever had my hand on such an expensive animal before!' The little bull stood sadly, taking no notice of us. The special Rhydygarnedd coarse mix lay untouched in his feeding bowl. 'He's poody yet' (upset, sulking), said Elwyn with a laugh, 'but he'll soon come happier.' He did. As soon as he met his lovely furry wives his eyes brightened, and life clearly took on a new dimension of interest for him.

The following October, the first of his calves was born. It was a bull calf, and we named it Gwynfor, for the Welsh Nationalist leader. I tried to make a pet of him, stealing cautiously up to rub his curly head as he lay in a little form in the lee of a clump of thistles, but wariness came with age, and by the time he was a week old he would not wait to be stroked. Other calves were born, and formed a wild play-group as soon as they felt the strength of their legs. For the first week or so of their lives a calf would stay very close to its mother, or rest where she had left it while she grazed close by. But they were independent little things at heart, and they soon seemed to gravitate to their own age group. Six or seven of them would be in one field, making babyish attempts to graze, perhaps, when suddenly a spirit of fun would invade the group and off they would all dash, bucking away with arched tails, and looking from a distance like a demented assembly of big black cats jumping over the tussocks.

A second generation of calves is skipping at Penllwynplan as I write, and the first lot are due for the market. We have been out of dairying for two years, and we are beginning to learn a little about the very different business of beef farming.

People often ask me if I would like to go back to milking, but I think the answer is probably no. The discipline was harder, although it often brought rewards as well. I remember going to fetch the cows for milking one May morning before seven o'clock. I was walking down the track with the sun coming over my shoulder when suddenly I saw a fox in the mowing grass on my left. He didn't see me, and for perhaps half a minute I watched him walking slowly along, not twenty feet away, turning his head this way and that to sniff the dew-jewelled grasses and flowers. Then he looked at me, and for a moment the sun shone straight into his golden eyes. I stood very still, but the dog came bustling up, so with a series of unhurried bounds my fox retired.

But even though I no longer get up to enjoy the break of day, single-suckler farming has its highlights. It is lovely to walk round the stock in November, when the fields are full of young calves; to feel the mild, damp air, and the spongy, yielding grass underfoot; to see the mink-like bloom on the leafless woods, and the sprays of gold where the hedgerow willows and hazels still hoard their coinage. You plan improvements as you walk round; this hedge should be laid this year, that gate repaired; a new water-trough might be put in here. One part of your mind is concentrated on the stock—what fine youngsters the bull is

144

siring, even better hindquarters than his own! but out of the corner of your eye you are aware of a party of long-tailed tits tossing like thistledown over the dark hedge. And it is nice to know that when you go into the house at dusk, your work is over for the day. No, I don't think I would go back to milking, dearly though I love Friesian cows.

THIRTEEN

WILDFLOWERS WITH
CONSEQUENCES

When we first came to Penllwynplan, there were some flower-beds in the garden, but we neglected them, and in a year or two, they grew over. We were feeling our way in our work then; we did everything slowly, and we were terribly conscientious. We used to get up at five, that first summer, and often we didn't come in for our supper at the end of the day's work until half past nine.

So for the first few years, if we wanted to look at flowers, we had to make do with wild ones. And somehow we found that, having got our eye in for them, they looked natural and right. It came as quite a surprise to me, attending a funeral in June of the fourth year, to see the graves in the churchyard all dressed with bunches of lupins and peonies. They looked grotesquely large—gross, almost, and flashy, to an eye now accustomed to campions and foxgloves.

The countryside around Meidrim is freely embroidered with wildflowers. Acres of snowdrops and wood anemones are succeeded by sheets of bluebells in the copses; daffodils—garden escapes, mostly, the Tenby daffodil rather than the Lent lily—star the hedge banks in April. The pageant of summer continues with sorrel, daisies, foxgloves, meadowsweet, orchids, valerian; to list them all would be to write a catalogue.

But Penllwynplan itself is not flowery. Just as our farm buildings are unfortunately totally unromantic, so our hedgerows and banks were merely green. A mile up the road I could show you a bank where the primroses grow in soft, generous tuffets; you could hardly put your foot down between them without crushing half a dozen flowers. But for some reason we had hardly any. Over the years I have discovered an individual here, a tiny colony there; but nothing that the most partisan judge could describe as abundance.

I did once try to remedy it by digging up half a dozen plants and dibbing them into a bank in my garden, but I am ashamed to say they died. Even then, I never dug up anything with an easy conscience. Even though he was far away, the figure of my father seemed to be standing behind me, looking over my shoulder. 'What if everybody did it?' the vision would say, beetling its brows. And the answer to that 'what if' is all too plain in what has happened in the South East of England; the primrose would soon cease to exist as a wild plant. Now it is illegal to dig things up, which is probably just as well.

I am however not without a stock of primroses. Year by year, I used to follow the fortunes of one fat clump that grew on the verge of the road that runs down to Meidrim. When the cows were grazing fields to which that road was the access, I would pass it eight times a day, going and coming. I should have liked to take it, but the memory of the earlier deaths held me back.

One spring day, however, a gang of council workmen arrived with shovels to neaten up the road verge. In their enthusiasm, they chopped about eighteen inches more turf than had ever been chopped before, and as I passed, I noticed that my primrose was right in the line of fire. Luckily, they didn't reach it that day, so I was able to sneak out with my trowel and a handy plastic bag, and carry it home to safety. I put it in a shady garden bed this time, with a lot of leafmould, and it took and prospered. It is now three times its original size, and I know that in a damp spell, I can divide it into about ten plants.

I have also made several attempts to grow primroses from seed, but in seed sowing I have an unfortunate touch of the brown thumb. I go through the motions—I watch, earnestly, as my father prepares seed trays and sows seeds therein. I use the same compost and seed from the same nursery. I would swear I do everything in exactly the same way. But somehow, everything he touches comes up like mustard and cress, whereas I usually end up with a panful of nothing. I have gone to the lengths of asking good seed sowers to take my packets and at least germinate them in their own house, but secure in the knowledge of their own skill, they can't believe that I can really mean it. 'But Elizabeth!' they say, reproachfully 'Of course they'll germinate if you do it correctly!'

I have had a few successes, but few indeed in proportion to my failures. But I keep on trying. And who knows? Perhaps the light will suddenly dawn and I will realise what it is that so often turns the cradle of my seeds into an early grave.

I often find that if I deeply smell a flower, or, say, the fragrant, resinous bud of the balsam poplar, the scent seems to stay in my nose for several hours. I keep getting, as it were, a reprise of it, which is nice. Similarly if I have been reading a bulb catalogue before milking, my mind seems to be full of shadowy leaves and petals, even though with the conscious part of it I am noticing that Meadowsweet is being slow *again* to milk out on that back left quarter, and wondering if the machine, perhaps, needs new teat-cup liners. I so enjoyed this bower of freshness inside my own head that I used to go to some trouble to put myself into the right frame of mind before milking. I used to imagine myself a situation—sometimes real, sometimes made up. It might be a wood or a hedge. Sometimes it would be a field corner, a sunny shoulder of turf running down to a quarter of an acre of rushy bog at the bottom. Then I would people it with wildflowers, according to its situation. This would keep my mind comfortably employed, with much delight, while the milking, like a wounded snake, dragged its slow length along. Soon the game got so absorbing that it could not be adequately contained in my head, along with all the other information of more practical importance, like how many pounds of cake should Atalanta be having, or that Daisy looks as if she will calve tonight. So I took to writing it down. There was always plenty of clean used paper cattle-cake bags to hand, and I used to tear off a big piece and keep it in the dairy, on the flat part of the bulk milk tank, with a stub of pencil. I did try putting it on the windowsill of the milking parlour itself, but it was apt to get eaten when my back was turned. When I was busy I would be thinking, and when there was a pause, all four machines safely on, nobody finished yet, I would nip into the dairy for half a minute and write my thoughts down. They usually took the form of lists, in order of flowering, of species appropriate to the particular setting I had given myself that day. Sternly factual as they were, the lists of flowers would fill my mind with amazed delight as I darted back to put the next four cows through the parlour, 'Celandines' my list might start; but that would give a good five-minutes' worth, and in my mind I would finger, with love, the juicy, brittle stems. The sturdiness of the celandine has always endeared it to me, and its forthrightness. It seems to come up looking so organised, with

148

its bright burnished disk. There is an inner ring of dimmer yellow at the base of the petals, and the brush of stamens completes the pattern of concentric circles. A bright healthy patch of celandines always makes me think of a William Morris design. The plants cunningly hug the contours of the banks they grow in, positioning themselves with a rightness that is hard to imitate when you come to plant a garden. The leaves are lovely too, surely as variously patterned as those of the much advertised neapolitan cyclamen, beloved of garden book writers.

I was amazed to find how long my lists became—how rich, by implication, was the material available to us in our own native species. Sometimes I kept my lists, but most of them got eaten, or blew away, or fell into a cowpat and had to be swept up and discarded. So I had the pleasure of making them many times over. The idea of them in my mind was like a sweet tucked in the cheek—at any time it could be brought into the foreground and made to yield its satisfactions.

While we were still dairying, I didn't do anything much about putting any of my ideas into practice. To make milking cows pay, you have to get as much milk as possible from grass, and cut down your bills for expensive cattle cake. Thus, you encourage your grass to start growing early in the spring, and do what you can to keep it growing late into the autumn. And this inevitably means putting artificial fertiliser onto it. Now wildflowers do not seem to like artificial fertilisers, and where a powerful diet of them is provided, they die. The things that love them, flourish on them, and utilise them to the best advantage, are the cultivated strains of grass that you put in when you re-seed a pasture. And to keep these strains dominant, in a pasture from which you are looking for really heavy grass production, you have to keep ploughing and re-seeding. How often you do it depends on your land and the kind of farming you are doing. But it appears that after, say, seven years, many of the original grasses sown in will have died, and their places have been taken by inferior grasses, weed grasses from the hedgerows, whose seeds have been scattered by the wind. So in goes the plough again, and any creeping wildflower that has managed to gain a foothold has another setback.

Of course not all fields are farmed on the 'ley system', as this regular re-seeding is called. There are fields which are too steep, too wet, or too rocky to lend themselves to ploughing. There is also a body of informed opinion that believes that permanent pasture, properly managed, can yield as much grass as a ley. But 'properly managed' in this context usually means lime and nitrogenous fertilisers, and constant defoliation by grazing animals, and that does not make a very happy environment for the average wildflower either.

I suppose in days gone by, when cowslips grew so thick in the meadows that nobody thought anything about them, there were actually fewer grazing animals in the country than there are now. Hard grazing in winter seems to kill out the cowslip, and in this part of the world at any rate, every blade of green that the earth will bear is utilised. Sheep are brought down from the mountains for the winter, paying their board and lodging on many lowland farms, and before they go home in April, they have laid the fields as bare as a plate. Grass can recover from this kind of usage, but for many wildflowers it is the last straw.

But when we sold off the dairy cows and brought in the Welsh Blacks, an opportunity for a more active line in conservation presented itself. As long as we were dairying, we had been looking for intensive production. Put-a-lot-in, get-a-lot-out had been the strategy, and heavy bills for cake, fertiliser, and grass-seed, had at least led to a fairly substantial monthly milk-cheque. But with the Blacks, we adopted a different plan. Their job was to produce a well-grown calf each year, with as little trouble and expense as possible. So no more milk was wanted than one calf could comfortably consume; and if possible, the flow should increase, rather than decrease, as he got bigger, and could use it better. The great flushes of grass that led the best of our Friesians to produce eight to ten gallons of milk a day would clearly be inappropriate; the muck from the hen-shed, steadily applied over the year, was all the fertiliser the grazing fields needed, and the cows' own dung, collected during the winter, would go to feed the silage fields. We arranged to have the calves born during the autumn, so that while they were little they could utilise the moderate flow of milk that their dams produced off autumn grazing and an ample winter diet of silage. In theory, the flush of grass in the spring should give the lactation an upward turn, and the calf, now perhaps four months old, should be able to utilise the extra milk so cheaply produced. Practice has a way of confounding theory, and we have not been running the system long enough to spot the flaws in it, but no doubt time will tell.

Conservation is a wide field, and it was, as I have written before, a chance conversation with a friend that narrowed my vague good intentions down to the point of actually doing something about it. We were talking about common wildflowers when he remarked, 'But what do you call a common wildflower now? For instance, when did you last see a cowslip?' And all of a sudden, everything seemed to come together—my lists, the need, the opportunity presented by our new way of farming. I decided there and then to try to make the farm a reserve, not for the obscure and recherché, but for the everyday flowers of the field and hedgerow. It turned out to be a lucky decision.

Of course in many ways I am totally unfitted for the task that I had undertaken. My warmest friends, in the kindness of their hearts, could never pretend that I am anything but disorganised. Bustling around and getting things moving is as foreign to me as space flight. My approach to life is rather more self-indulgent; I think about things for a long time; I drift; I potter. But one of the beauties of an enterprise you have initiated yourself is that nobody can tell you you are doing it wrong. At least in the early, private stages, it is your own thing. So I went about it in my own way, taking seeds of this and cuttings of that, sticking them in the garden for safe keeping, and learning from my mistakes as I went along.

A pure chance, resulting from something quite unconnected with wildflower conservation, gave me substantial encouragement in the first summer. In one of our fields, called the Dip, there is a concrete trough, fed by a spring that comes out of the hillside. Dependent as we were for our water supply on two hideously temperamental wells, we could never afford to let the cows drink tap water in the summer. They had to get what they needed from the spring. This did not present any very serious difficulties; the Dip is in the middle of the farm, like the middle of a buttercup, with the other fields lying around like petals. So it was easy, whatever field we were grazing, to let them have a run back to the Dip, to get access to the trough of clear, cold water. The Dip was unimportant agriculturally; too steep sided to be safe for the tractor, it had never been fertilised or re-seeded, and the cows, with permanent access, kept it shaved like a bowling green.

But in the spring of that year, after many months of stately consideration, the Council agreed to lay mains water to our

151

farm. The tapping was brought on to our land in the bottom corner, nearest to the village, and the first thing we installed there was a drinking trough. So for the first time in ten summers, the gate to the Dip was closed, and the close-bitten wild turf there had a chance to show what it was made of. As it turned out, it was mostly made of flowers. An astonishing array of purple, gold, pink, ivory and powder blue sprang up, like some rich oriental carpet. I was reminded of a grass tennis court I had once read about, which for twenty years was in use, and was kept closely mown. In the twenty-first year of its owners' incumbency, however, there came a great drought. The grass stopped growing, and mowing was suspended for a couple of months. Great was everybody's amazement when at the end of that time, the tennis court was suddenly spangled all over with the flowers of some wild orchis. The plants must have been there all the time, regularly snubbed by the mower, and patiently trying again, until after twenty years the opportunity came to declare themselves. So our Dip showed us what it could do. If we were willing to give it June and July to itself to do it in.

The obvious inference to draw from this lucky disclosure was that as far as the flowers growing among the grass in the business part of a field were concerned, they would have to be arranged in some kind of seasonal sequence. Thus, it is clearly no use introducing cowslips and Lent lilies into the fields where you are hoping for a March bite for your cattle. Cattle are hungry for anything green at that time of the year, and would soon reduce everything to sward level. The obvious place for the early spring flat-field dwellers must be in the hay or silage fields, where they can hopefully flower and set their seed, or make their bulb, before the crop is cut.

Other species are by their nature bank dwellers, and after a year or two of experiment I have come to the conclusion that there is no easy way of protecting them. If you let your stock have access to the banks, the flowers get eaten; if you erect a single-strand fence to keep them at bay, you are left with the problem of trashing off the rough growth by hand at the end of the summer. Probably the ideal solution would be to have some kind of movable fence, a really good electric fence, probably a mains one, so that when the desired species had seeded, the cattle could be allowed to get at the bank and do the trashing for you. Clearly it is not a problem beyond the ingenuity of man to solve;

probably the answer just lies in being willing to spend a little money.

Really, what I am trying to do is a kind of large-scale gardening with wild species. My notebook is full of jotted-down suggestions for plant associations, for example:

'July 20th, still hot and dry. Meadowsweet and honeysuckle both flowering, cream and warm pinky-yellow, would look good together.' Some people have already succeeded at some times of the year in what I am trying to do. A bank alongside the farm drive of some friends of ours, for instance, is a total success in spring. Snowdrops, celandines and Tenby daffodils, are the early stars, coming before the leaves, while the bank is quite sunny. Later, when the overarching sycamores begin to dapple it with shade, clumps of primroses appear. Azure bluebells and deep magenta early purple orchis give strong notes of colour, while the lacy cow-parsley adds an airy grace to the picture. I hope to find a suitable bank to reproduce this planting-picture somewhere at Penllwynplan.

This summer (1975) on a visit to the Gower, it struck me that a very similar effect could perhaps be made with flowers that would come to their peak in July. On the sandy burrows, sheets of harebells nodded their large single flowers, in a fairly similar shade of campanula-blue to the bluebell—at any rate, at a distance; geranium sanguineum rambled happily around, with flowers of the same rich magenta as the orchis. I was puzzled for a while to find the primrose element until my eye lighted upon the jolly toadflax straggling up the hedge. Its lip is orange, it is true; but the general effect is of a pale yellow flower not at all dissimilar to the colour of the primrose. With the permission of the owner of the land, I collected a plant each of the harebell and the geranium—toadflax I have in abundance—and when they have grown a bit more stalwart in the garden, I shall adventure them out together on some protected bank.

Keeping notes of what flowers are out at any one time suggests plant associations. The foxgloves look pretty with red clover or campions growing near them, and when it struck me one day that a distant smudge of willow herb was exactly the same colour as foxgloves, I wondered what to encourage to grow with it, as a complementary plant. Then, driving to Carmarthen, I noted automatically that the common pink mallow was flowering away on the embankments of the new double carriage way, and the problem solved itself. I got some mallow seed and sowed it; my evil genius did its stuff, and only one seed germinated, but at least it looks a nice healthy little plant, and I shall introduce it to its destined dancing-partner next spring.

One lucky day, when I had been potching along in this way for some time, my eye was caught by an announcement of a competition in the *Sunday Times*. 'Kenneth Allsop Memorial Essay' it said, and went on to offer a prize of £250 for an essay of up to 1,200 words on any subject connected with conservation. 'I suppose I could write about the flower reserve,' I thought, and clipped out the cutting—noting, mistakenly, as it turned out, that entries had to be submitted by the end of October.

I thought about the essay from time to time, and even went so far as to imagine what I might write; but having ordered my life for many years on the principle of 'never do today what you can put off till tomorrow' I actually *did* nothing about it. The 30th October came and went, and I thought to myself 'Fool! You've missed your chance.'

Then the *Sunday Times* published a little reminder that said brightly 'Only 15 days now to complete and send in your entries for the Kenneth Allsop Memorial Essay, which must reach this office by Saturday November 30th,' and I realised that I was being offered a second chance. I have always had a superstitious feeling about a second chance; to let idleness win again would be to plant a singularly ungrateful kick in the teeth of fate, and I resolved that, come what might, I would write the essay, and send it off in time. I wrote the first page.

On the Monday of the last week, I still had not done any more. I looked ahead and designated Thursday afternoon as essay-writing time. But when it came, and I sat down, I found that the page I had already done was useless, and tore it up. Then the cattle burst out, and I had to help Desmond to chase them back over miles of sodden Welsh countryside, and to re-make the considerable portion of the fence that they had disrupted, before it got dark. That evening, someone came to see us, so my page remained virgin still.

On Friday at lunch-time, I said 'I am as deaf as an adder to the world until this essay is in the post. If the cattle get out, they can stay out for me. If anybody comes for eggs, they can help themselves as far as I am concerned. All I ask is that nobody speaks to me until I've finished it. Read it if you like, but please

154

don't tell me anything that's the matter with it, because there won't be time to alter it *and* catch the post at half past four.'

So Desmond and Rachel sat in grim silence, reading with careful absence of commentary each page as it flipped from the pile of paper in front of me. Even their faces were expressionless —which I couldn't grumble at, as it was after all exactly what I'd asked for. It gave the whole affair a curiously portentous atmosphere—as if it was a matter of life and death.

It was just about four o'clock when I finished, and came back into communication with the world. Rachel found me a long envelope, Desmond drove us down to the village, where we stuck on a first class stamp, and dropped it into the mail box with ten minutes to spare before the last post went. It was up to the post office now.

Everybody else soon forgot about it, but every Sunday I secretly searched for an announcement. It wasn't that I expected to win; that would have been presumptuous. But I was a bit afraid the others *might* think I was expecting to win if they saw me looking. So every Sunday, I took my opportunity when I could, before anybody else was up, to search through the *Sunday Times* quite minutely.

Week followed week, and there was nothing. Christmas came and went, and I began to think I must have missed the announcement. The celandines gilded the hedge, and still, almost from habit, I looked. And then one day in early March I found it. I was kneeling on the kitchen floor, the better to get the whole paper spread out, and there was a discreet little paragraph which said, unbelievably 'The winner of this year's Kenneth Allsop Memorial Essay Competition is Mrs. Elizabeth Cragoe of Carmarthen.'

'Desmond! Desmond!' I shouted squeakily. 'Look at this!' 'Um, um, what is it, I'll look at it later,' murmured Desmond, who was deep in a perusal of the leading article. But when I thrust it remorselessly under his nose and he saw what it was, he was as delighted as I was.

It was great fun having lots of people come up to me in the market and say, 'I saw your name in the paper the other day. Congratulations!' One tiny cloud dimmed the horizon. In the original announcement it had said 'Winners will be notified by letter', and now day followed day, and I hadn't heard anything. Was I living on stolen glory? Could there possibly be another

Mrs. Elizabeth Cragoe in Carmarthen who had gone in for the same competition? But on the Saturday following the announcement the letter arrived, complete with the lovely cheque, and my lingering fears were set at rest.

Everybody was tremendously nice about it. The *Sunday Times* wanted a photograph to publish with the article, and Hunter Davies, the section editor, asked me to make it one of all of us. 'I'm a sucker for a family photograph,' he said. So a photographer came down, and we all arranged to have haircuts and clean sweaters for the big day. As it was during the Easter holidays, both the children were at home. The photographer wanted a flowery background, to be in keeping with the subject of the essay, but we had had the cows out all winter, and there was hardly a blade of grass, let alone a flower, on the mudpocked battlefield that was Penllwynplan. So we piled into two cars including some friends who were staying with us for Easter, and who came to see the sport, and went off up the lane in search of Flora.

We found a south facing bank studded with clumps of early primroses, and we pressed ourselves against that for a few shots. Then we noticed a daisy-sprinkled patch of grass in a field, so we all went and squatted on that. 'I'd better get a few upright shots in case the shape fits better on the page,' said the photographer, and conducting us to the edge of the field, he compressed us painfully into a narrow niche between two tall flowering gorse bushes. Torn, bleeding, and blue with cold, we begged him to call it a day, but when we got back to Penllwynplan his eye lighted on the fading snowdrops spilling over the bank beside the road. 'Just one more' he said. 'As it'll be a black-and-white picture, this might be the best background of all.' It was, in fact, the one they used.

The essay was duly published, with a little editorial note that, I must say, caused me a certain amount of embarrassment. It said that Desmond and I had been city people who had decided to put it all behind us, and 'farm as nearly as possible as nature intended.' This caused riotous mirth among those who know that we make most of our living from battery hens, and one witty man pressed into my hand a scrap of paper with this written on it:

'To be sung, slowly and with expression, to the tune of America, from West Side Story.

Farming is Fun down at Penllwynplan;
Ecology's King down at Penllwynplan;
Back to Nature's the Right Way, Man,
Unless you're a Hen, down at Penllwynplan!'

I like it, I like it.

I had a couple of short interviews for radio programmes, which I enjoyed, though I found myself surprisingly nervous and breathless, considering that I wasn't facing anything more awe-inspiring than a tape recorder. One or two journalists came to interview me too, and I had several charming letters from *Sunday Times* readers who had read the essay. Many of them offered me plants, which I accepted gratefully, and I received a tremendous boost to my stock, both in kinds and in numbers.

But the most exciting thing of all was a letter, which arrived one morning. It was from a literary agent, who had read the essay, and wondered if I would like to write a book about our farming experiences, and have him represent it for me. Naturally, I didn't hesitate to accept this wonderful opportunity, and the very next time I went down to the market, I bought a blue notebook for 6p, and began making notes of subject matter for various chapters.

I made a slow start, writing with difficulty, and discarding a lot of what I first produced. My mother often used to say when I was young 'Real writers can't *help* writing. They write all the time. Writing is all they want to do.' It wasn't a bit like that with me, and I felt quite encouraged when a friend told me the working mottoes of two famous authors whom she happened to know. 'Every word produced in pain' was how one described his work, while the other one said 'It's dogged as does it'. That was much more like it, and further encouragement came when my agent, to whom I had duly sent a sample chapter and a synopsis of the book, wrote to say that he had found me a publisher. I had to do it now.

Nothing acts as such a spur as a little bit of compulsion, and when I took the children for a caravan holiday in the Gower in the summer, I found that words were beginning to flow more easily.

I still feel dissatisfied with what I write, and wish I could express myself better. But now I have nearly completed a book,

I am beginning to enjoy writing, and I can feel the next seven or so books standing in line inside my head behind my brow, waiting their turn to be written. I wonder if they will ever get out? Only time will tell.

FOURTEEN

SO FAR SO GOOD

When I get on my hobby-horse on the subject of living in the country I have to be careful not to sound too much like nauseous Pollyanna, playing the Glad Game. Born and partly raised in a big, black conurbation, I still feel all the force of the good fortune that has enabled me to become a farmer. Sometimes, in spring, I feel so happy to be where I am that I could almost go down on my knees and eat grass like the cows. I don't, of course; experience indicates that such extravagant gestures only end in bathos, like accidentally biting an earthworm, or getting a beetle in your mouth. But I do feel that I would like to make some kind of acknowledgement of the agreeableness of my circumstances.

'What about your *cultural* life?' friends ask, cautiously. But geography doesn't do much to limit culture in these days, and such cultural life as we do have is actually richer, I think, than it was when we lived near London. It isn't so much that there is more available, as that we make more use of what there is.

There is an excellent public library in Carmarthen, housed in a beautiful restored eighteenth-century building; the travelling library comes to our very gate once a fortnight, and shows the most Christian forbearance in its attitude to the number of books you can have out, or the number of weeks you can keep them.

Live music is a fairly rare treat unless you want to go twenty miles to Swansea, but there are recitals sometimes, and we can go about once a year to a performance by the Welsh National Opera Company, which sends round travelling offshoots to do one-night stands in the smaller towns like Carmarthen. Wales is the land of choirs, of course, and concerts of a wonderfully high standard are often put on.

For my money, I get most pleasure from listening to music in the peace and quiet of my own drawing-room, on the gramo-phone. One is distracted in the concert hall by other people's sniffing, coughing and fidgeting. You can't choose the pro-gramme, and besides, my concentration won't stretch at the most profitable level of intensity for more than one major work. We bought ourselves a nice gramophone a couple of years ago, and what with records that we borrow from the library and our own stock (constantly augmented by the excellent second-hand ones that we buy in the market; whoever can it be who keeps wanting to sell them?) there is almost an *embarras de richesses* when you go to choose something to listen to.

Wales has always been in the forefront in matters of education, and there are vigorous and well-attended evening classes for those who want them. I have been to classes in cookery, upholstery, and music appreciation; pottery and local history are on the list of ones I still want to do.

Having been a town person, I still feel a great delight in things that are as normal as breathing to our Welsh neighbours. Log fires, for instance; both the thought and the actuality. The thought that you can warm your house from the excess of your own hedgerow timber if you want to, using only what grows again, and making up by generous planting what you remove as a harvest—is ecologically satisfying. However the scientists may be working on harnessing the energy of the winds, the tides and the sun for man's use, it is still frightening to think of our wild and reckless depletion of the earth's fossil fuels. Burning wood is making use of the sun's power too; the leaves spread wide in the light, photosynthesising away, make the plantfoods that build the timber, and the stored warmth is released in the ever-changing glow of our deep brick hearth. 'Who needs television when you can sit and look at a log fire?' asked one of our friends, a great country-lover, stretching out his hands to the glow. This so much echoes what I feel about it that I quoted it to a neigh-bour. 'The only trouble with that as I see it,' he replied, 'is that it's the same programme every night!' I conclude that you have to be town-born to be a romantic!

There is at the moment a substantial movement among people who, like us, have come from the towns to live in the country, towards self-sufficiency. Living off your own land, farming organically, and taking out nothing that you can't put back are its tenets. There is something quite appealing about the idea in theory, and sometimes I feel drawn to it, but I think that in practice it is *too* romantic, and takes no account of the real nature of our modern situation.

The fact that the body gets old is one problem. In your twenties your physique easily surmounts the hard facts of self-sufficient life. You fell trees and saw up logs easily, rejoicing in the beautiful interplay of saw and muscle, craft and strength. But perhaps when you are fifty, and you have hurt your back a bit, and it won't come right, and you are the man of the family, and if you don't saw the logs—a good lot of logs—nobody can have a fire, it doesn't seem quite so good. The hopefuls say that by then there should be younger men coming on; but we should not try to constrain other people into our way of life to suit our own convenience; maybe the young ones will want to be off. Another answer is to form some kind of commune, but the only communes I have seen in action seem to divide their time among squalid squabblings, gazings into the murky recesses of their own little souls, and queueing up at the dole office.

The history of civilisation is really the history of specialisation, and to be properly self-sufficient you have to be the very antithesis of a specialist. All forms of progress have happened because people have acquired spare time, as technical innovations have eased the sheer hard grind of staying alive. The would-be self-sufficients seek to reverse this trend, but if they are true to their image, it cannot be long before all their delight in their life's simplicity is bogged down in a mire of drudgery.

What actually happens is that they avail themselves of the fringe benefits of the big industrial civilisation that they affect to despise. The very saw with which they cut up their logs is made of the finest steel, manufactured in Sheffield or perhaps Bremen. When it gets blunt, they take it to the hardware shop in town to get it sharpened and re-set. In effect, they are only able to live in the country in reasonable comfort because there are other people living in towns, manufacturing the equipment that makes it possible for them to do so.

People on a doctrinaire self-sufficiency kick get up my nose. I think they stand convicted of mental dishonesty. But I have all the time in the world for people who acknowledge that they have come to live in the country because they like it—who acknowledge that they are lucky to be here, rather than implying that they are morally superior because they have left the flesh-pots.

161

Of course growing your own food, whether it be stock, cereals, or fruit and vegetables, is fun, albeit time consuming. We have had some quite successful seasons of vegetable gardening; other years we don't seem to find the time. Having started our business by the grace of the Bank Manager on an overdraft, we have been committed to a money economy from the beginning, and I am not altogether sorry. Having good dollops of repayment to make to the bank does keep you up to a reasonable standard of efficiency. Desmond was born efficient, but I might easily have strayed down the most wayward paths of crankiness without the financial constraints of our circumstances.

There have been times when money has been really tight indeed, and we have lain in bed at nights sweating with anxiety about our commitments. When we were hard pressed like that I used sometimes to think of the jolly ditty sung to the tune of 'My bonny lies over the ocean', that starts:

> My father makes counterfeit money,
> My mother makes synthetic gin. . . .

and ends with a roaring chorus of 'My God, how the money rolls in!' It often seemed that our industry, farming, albeit fundamental, must be one of the worst paid in the world. But reviewing all the money-making alternatives that the song offered, none of them seemed particularly attractive. We were still glad we had chosen to be farmers rather than illicit distillers, counterfeiters, or something worse.

It is a truism to say that life is cyclical, but in that fact lies much of the satisfaction of farming and living a country life. The ever-widening pattern of recurrent cycles—each day, with its pleasant round of familiar work, each week, following a pre-ordained course, each year, with its changing seasons, shows up more clearly in the country than in the town. Antitheses balance one another with the correctness of a formal dance. Day-night. Spring-autumn. Work-rest. Shortage-plenty. Youth-age. Death-life. The saving-up-for and buying of a farm, the creation of a viable business, the getting it all as you want it, and the fruition of your efforts (with luck) constitute a cycle that takes a whole lifetime. Adding in the slow creation of a flower reserve makes it even more certain that we shall never suffer from that pettish feeling of not having anything worthwhile to do.

No one is so naive of course, nowadays, as to think that he is building for posterity. Your own farm, forest, garden, or what you will, is yours for a life's duration only; whoever gets it next has as much right to change it as you did, and it won't do to kick against the pricks. A large house quite near this farm belonged in the latter part of the last century to a much-travelled man who loved exotic plants. He flourished in the great age of botanical exploration, and he planted the park and gardens of the mansion with the choicest selection of trees and shrubs that he could procure, freshly imported from China and the Himalayas. The plants grew well, and connoisseurs came from far away to see them and admire. But all flesh is grass, and when the original owner died, the property was bought by an ordinary farmer, with no aesthetic thoughts higher than his cheque book. Looking at the gingkoes he thought 'Fencing-posts!' and regarding the sequoias he said 'Building-timber!' And so it was, and now all that remains of that once notable collection is a wood with a few rhododendron species growing in it, and one solitary Wellingtonia, in front of the house. So it will probably be with my wild-flower reserve. But why should I repine? I shall have had the pleasure of making it.

It is curious how, to many people born and living in towns, comes this strong feeling that farming, or at any rate living in the country, is real life—true living, as opposed to just existing. I think, myself, that farming offers a human being an optimal chance to develop a whole personality.

A rural circle automatically restricts the number of people you know; the image of your own identity is faceted back to you by a comprehensibly small number of friends and acquaintances. You have a recognised place in the community, unlike a man in a big city. His beam of self is not reflected back to him by the people he meets; most of them are strangers, and the self that he projects is largely dissipated and lost, diffused by being bounced off too many refractive surfaces too randomly presented in the seething crowds he goes among every day.

Farming gives you time, as well as space, to be yourself. Your work automatically brings you fresh air and exercise, so you feel well most of the time. Indigestion and insomnia, the curses of the twentieth century, do not much trouble farmers. You feel the satisfaction of exercising a craft skill when you lay a hedge, do up a pretty heifer to sell, or even truss a neat chicken. And

163

in the rhythmic peace of routine jobs like milking or collecting eggs, when the conscious part of your mind is partly in abeyance, ideas sometimes swim up out of your subconscious like big carp coming to the surface of a pool. I won't pretend that they are ever more than half-baked commonplaces, but at least they are your own, which provides a certain satisfaction.

'Don't make it sound too nice,' said somebody to me, recently. 'You know hardly anybody can afford to get a start in farming these days.' But I am convinced that in spite of the jump in the value of land, and the hard times farmers have been through in the last few years, it is still perfectly possible for a person without much capital to get a start on the land. A young couple who were willing to work and save up, say, a couple of thousand pounds could, with the help of a mortgage or bank loan, get themselves a derelict cottage and a few acres of land. They would have to be willing to work early and late, to put off having children for a few years, and not to spend any money on themselves, but the fact is that if you haven't got much capital, work and self-denial are the only substitutes.

Lots of envelopes have gone into the dustbin at Penllwynplan covered with the figures of budgets, worked out in detail, for cottage economies in my writing. The really important thing, I am sure, in trying to develop a business that will enable you to become a farmer with almost no capital, is to bend to what the world wants rather than following your own whim. In other words, you must make sure that you produce on your holding only things you know you can sell, instead of concentrating on what you like doing yourself, and then complaining because nobody will give you money for it. You must do your market research before you invest a penny.

What, then, could my imaginary couple produce on their few stony acres, that would enable them to pay their mortgage, live, and improve their property to the point where they could sell it and get something bigger?

The first point is not actually what they would produce, but how they would sell it when it was produced. At all costs they must avoid the middleman, and keep for themselves the full profits that will accrue from the sweat of their brows. 'Vertical Integration' was a favourite catch phrase in farming about ten years ago; for big farmers this presumably means developing food processing plant, and retail outlets for their produce. For the small, even the tiny, operator, it means making sure that the food you sell goes directly to the person who is going to eat it. In other words, he must have a mail order business, a market stall, a delivery round, or a farm shop.

'But I want to do farming, not marketing' some would-be farmers have said to me, making a pouting lip and kicking petulantly at a stone in the yard. Tough luck! Canute showed his courtiers that the tide wouldn't go back for telling, and the economics of farming are the same. The situation is as it is, and you have two options: either you accept it, and make the best use you can of it, or you ignore it, and then (usually) it gets you down.

Once my imaginary people have come to terms with the idea of selling their own produce direct, there is no end to the variety of the things they can grow, and most of them can be started in a small way and built up gradually. Eggs, honey, dressed rabbits, dressed chickens, all find a ready market. Vegetables, particularly if organically grown, show a high margin, although they are expensive in effort. Farm-churned butter can be sold for about 50p a pound, and in the holiday season, packed in the sort of round container soft margarine comes in, and prettily printed with an old wooden butter-stamp, the tourists would certainly buy all you could produce. Feed costs for stock could be expensive, but a good patch of potatoes and an acre of barley, with extra protein from the buttermilk after the churning, could fatten a pig or two, and cockerels, and rabbits. Rabbits could eat trimmings from vegetables raised for sale. Even parsley, at 10p a bunch, could provide a steady little income through nine months of the year, even more perhaps with luck and a plastic cloche. Top-quality soft fruit, carefully picked and punneted, would soon find an appreciative clientele, and cartons of fresh or clotted cream could be offered in season, as long as the buildings and water supply on the smallholding complied with the dairy regulations. Herbs, dried or growing in pots do not take up much room on a smallholding. Things for the dedicated flower-arranger, glycerined foliage, teazles and Chinese lanterns, might return a few pounds for a very small outlay. A gardening speciality, like ground-cover plants, could be built up for pence rather than pounds in the way of capital investment, and if there was any time over, a few really delicious home-made cakes might bring a few new faces round the stall. In Wales, where there is a tradition of keeping churchyards cared-for, cut flowers at reasonable prices can usually be sold, for putting on graves. The trick is not to depend too heavily on any one item, and to keep your costs down by growing everything, and its food, on your own place. It goes without saying, of course, that a meticulous attention to the quality of the produce is a must. The bitten lettuce, the burned cake, the torn chicken, you can eat yourselves.

If my young couple were hardworking and reasonably lucky, they would in six or seven years have repaired their cottage, tidied up their place, and be in a position to move to a bigger holding—perhaps about forty acres—with a nucleus of stock, implements, and experience.

This idyllic plan is of course very different from the one we followed ourselves. Our system is like the one I have outlined for them only in that it too offers an almost infinite perspective for more and more intensification, if one were willing to do the work. We already sell eggs and dressed end-of-lay poultry. We could, if we chose, rear our own chicks, and mill-and-mix our own feedstuffs. We could dry and process the hen manure, and sell it in bags as a garden fertiliser. We could cook and mince the discarded bits of the dressed poultry, and sell them as petfood. We could branch out into processed meats with birds that are too small to be worth selling oven-ready, and sell pressed chicken, chicken pie, and pâté. We could fatten all our own Welsh Black steers, have them slaughtered, and sell the meat wholesale to people for their deep freezes. We could set our vegetable garden growing again, and sell lettuces, radishes, and runner beans on our market stall. We do not do all these things because we like a little bit of leisure round the edges of our working day, and at the moment we seem to have enough to live on without them. But the opportunities are there.

We came to Meidrim twelve years ago, full of our theoretical knowledge, bolstered by many illusions, and hoping for the best. Many of our ideas have altered now. Practical experience has changed our perspective, and a mixed crop of successes and failures has made us more cautious in embracing new and revolutionary methods. I hope I can say that we are a little wiser now than we were when we came.

But when you say 'wiser', convention demands that you should say 'sadder' as well. After twelve years earning our living as farmers, I look inwards for that chastening of the spirit that is implied in the phrase. Do I feel sadder after twelve years as a farmer? No, I can put my hand on my heart and aver outright that it has not made me any sadder than I was.

In fact, not sad at all.